Aiming for Level
Writing
6

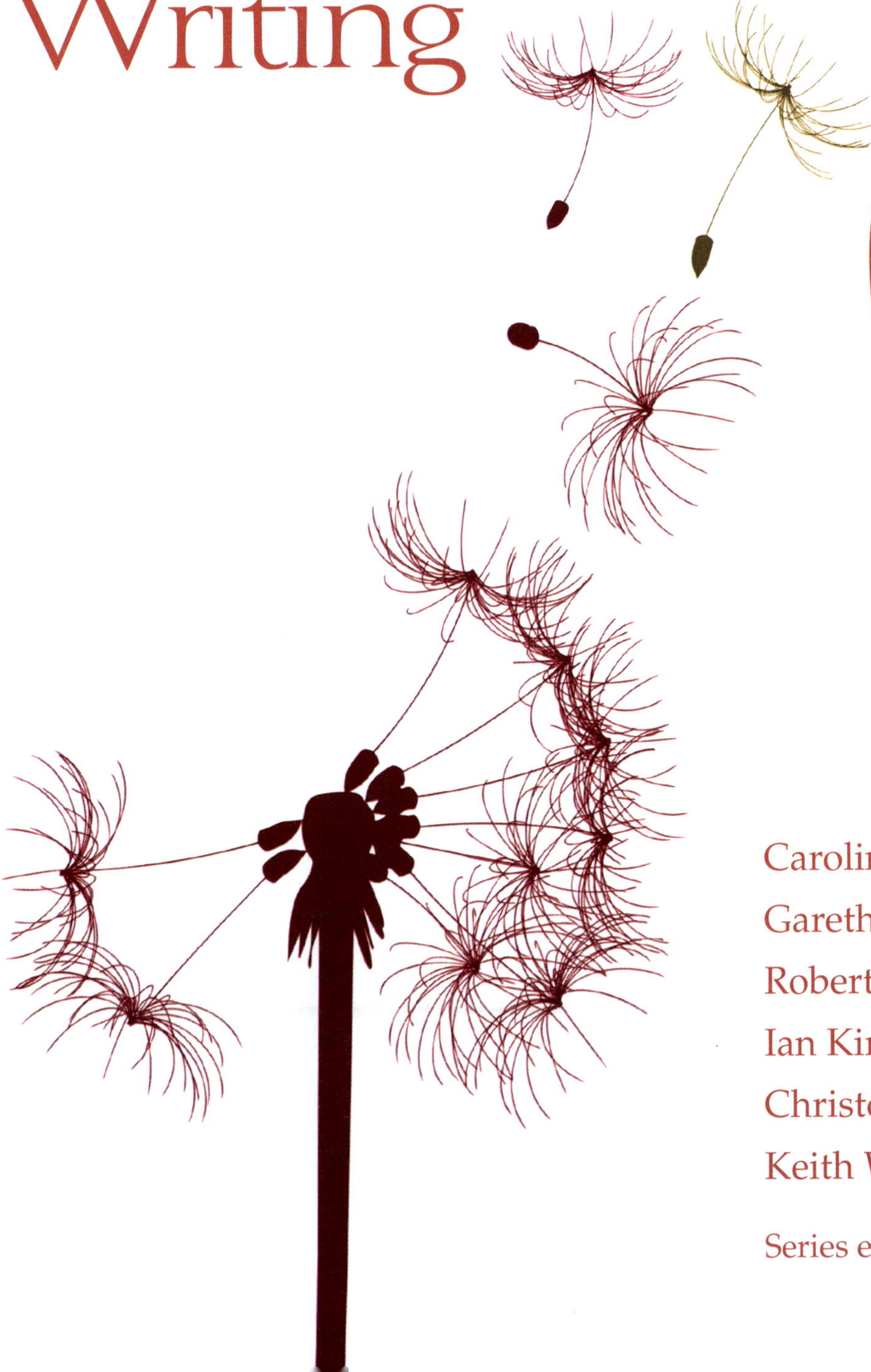

Caroline Bentley-Davies
Gareth Calway
Robert Francis
Ian Kirby
Christopher Martin
Keith West

Series editor: Gareth Calway

William Collins' dream of knowledge for all began with the publication of his first book in 1819. A self-educated mill worker, he not only enriched millions of lives, but also founded a flourishing publishing house. Today, staying true to this spirit, Collins books are packed with inspiration, innovation and practical expertise. They place you at the centre of a world of possibility and give you exactly what you need to explore it.

Collins. Freedom to teach.

Published by Collins
An imprint of HarperCollins Publishers
77-85 Fulham Palace Road
Hammersmith
London
W6 8JB

Browse the complete Collins catalogue at
www.collinseducation.com

© HarperCollins Publishers Limited 2009

10 9 8 7 6 5 4 3 2 1
ISBN 978 0 00 731361 7

Caroline Bentley-Davies, Gareth Calway, Robert Francis, Ian Kirby, Christopher Martin and Keith West assert their moral rights to be identified as the authors of this work.

All rights reserved. No part of this publication may be reproduced, stored in a retrieval system, or transmitted in any form or by any means, electronic, mechanical, photocopying, recording or otherwise, without the prior written permission of the Publisher or a licence permitting restricted copying in the United Kingdom issued by the Copyright Licensing Agency Ltd, 90 Tottenham Court Road, London W1T 4LP.

British Library Cataloguing in Publication Data.
A Catalogue record for this publication is available from the British Library.

Commissioning by Catherine Martin
Design and typesetting by Jordan Publishing Design
Cover Design by Angela English
Printed and bound by Martins the Printers

With thanks to Jo Kemp, Gemma Wain, Keith West and Ashley Lodge.

Acknowledgements

The publishers gratefully acknowledge the permissions granted to reproduce the copyright material in this book. While every effort has been made to trace and contact copyright holders, where this has not been possible the publishers will be pleased to make the necessary arrangements at the first opportunity.

Extracts from *The Lady in the Lake* by Raymond Chandler, published by Penguin Books Ltd. (pp6, 7); extracts from *Solo 1: Monologues for Drama* by John Goodwin and Bill Taylor, published by Hodder & Stoughton Publishers (pp8, 9); extract from *The Catcher in the Rye* by JD Salinger, published by Penguin Books Ltd. (p10); 'He Wishes for the Cloths of Heaven' by WB Yeats, © AP Watt (p18); extract from 'Misadventure in South-west China' by Tim Nolen, in *Lonely Planet Unpacked – Travel Disaster Stories*, published by Lonely Planet Publications (p20); extract from an article in *Daily Mail*, 6 Nov 08 © Solo Syndication 2008 (p22); extract from an article by Gill Hornby in *The Telegraph* 9 Mar 09 © The Telegraph Group 2009 (pp24-5); extract from an article by Kathy Marks in *The Independent* 10 Mar 09 (p26); extract from *Skeleton Key* by Anthony Horowitz, published by Walker Books Ltd. (p27); extract from *Stone Cold* by Joe Standerline, published by Nelson Thornes (pp30-1); extract from *Z for Zachariah* by Robert O. Brien, published by Puffin Books, part of Penguin Books Ltd. (p36); article by Lucy Hagan from *The Sun*, 29 Dec 08 © NI Syndication 2008 (p38); extract adapted from *Monologues with Duologue Activities*, published by First and Best in Education (p44); extract written by Mike Gould (p45); extract from *Death of a Hero* by Richard Aldington, published by Hogarth Press (p55); extracts from *The Woman in Black* by Susan Hill, published by Vintage Classics (pp56, 57, 59); extract from *Animal Farm* by George Orwell, published by Penguin Books Ltd. (pp61); extract from 'Turn of the World' in *The World and Other Places* by Jeanette Winterson, published by Vintage (p66); extract from *The Cloning of Joanna May* by Fay Weldon, published by HarperCollins Publishers (p66); extract from *The Boy Who Kicked Pigs* by Tom Baker, published by Faber & Faber (p68); extract from 'Tokyo Pastoral' in *Shaking a Leg* by Angela Carter, published by Vintage (p68); extract from *Casino Royale* by Ian Fleming, published by Penguin Books Ltd. (p69).

The publishers would like to thank the following for permission to reproduce pictures in these pages.

Alamy (pp10, 18, 20, 44, 60, 66b); Bridgeman Art Library (pp42, 45); change 4 life (p37); Getty Images (pp7, 8b, 14, 21, 24, 56); istockphoto (pp6, 19, 26, 30, 36, 48, 49, 50, 54, 59, 64, 66t, 74-5); Leeds College of Art and Design/Sorrell Foundation/Andy Edwards (p51t); Little, Brown (p11); Moviestore Collection (p58); Rex Features (pp8t, 22, 32, 34, 3946, 47, 69); Ronald Grant Archive (p61); Sorrell Foundation (p51b).

Contents

Chapter 1 — **AF1 Write imaginative, interesting and thoughtful texts** — 5
1. Write with a clear emphasis on narration rather than plot — 6
2. Write in character sustaining a role or voice — 8
3. Write in a form and style that achieves the right effect — 10
4. Write using a range of stylistic devices to create effects — 12
5. Make a good attempt to be creative with form — 14

Chapter 2 — **AF2 Produce texts which are appropriate to task, reader and purpose** — 17
1. Write imaginatively thinking about audience and purpose — 18
2. Use a range of techniques to create effects — 20
3. Write persuasively for a particular audience — 22
4. Adapt what you have read for different purposes — 26

Chapter 3 — **AF3 Organise and present whole texts effectively** — 29
1. Effectively control and sequence your work, thinking about the reader's reaction — 30
2. Use a range of features to signal the text's direction to the reader — 34
3. Develop clear and effective introductions — 36
4. Manage information, ideas and events to maximise the effect on the reader — 38

Chapter 4 — **AF4 Construct paragraphs and use cohesion** — 41
1. Write an intriguing opening paragraph — 42
2. Use paragraphs to create a unity of theme in fiction — 44
3. Create a unity of theme in non-fiction — 46
4. Use bridges to link ideas between paragraphs — 48
5. Improve your ability to shape ideas into cohesive paragraphs — 50

Chapter 5   **AF5** Vary sentences for clarity, purpose and effect
                   AF6 Write with technical accuracy of syntax and punctuation   53

       1 Shape sentences for effect   54
       2 Write expressive and varied sentences in exciting descriptive writing   56
       3 Write effective dialogue in stories and scripts   58
       4 Use rhetorical devices to make an impact   60

Chapter 6   **AF7** Select appropriate and effective vocabulary   63

       1 Develop a varied, ambitious vocabulary   64
       2 Use vocabulary with subtlety and originality   66
       3 Choose vocabulary that is appropriate to your audience and purpose   68

Chapter 7   **AF8** Use correct spelling   71

       1 Identify the building blocks of words   72
       2 Improve your spelling of ambitious, complex words   74

Teacher Guide   77

Chapter 1

AF1 Write imaginative, interesting and thoughtful texts

This chapter is going to show you how to

- Write with a clear emphasis on narration rather than plot
- Write in character sustaining a role or voice
- Write in a form and style that achieves the right effect
- Write using a range of stylistic devices to create effects
- Make a good attempt to be creative with form.

What's it all about?

It's very important to write in an imaginative and thoughtful way, choosing the right form and style and/or finding your own voice. This will give your writing aptness, interest and personality.

1 Write with a clear emphasis on narration rather than plot

This lesson will
- help you to add some crackle and zip to your writing.

'It's the way he tells them!' The best stories are about **the way they are told** – the **narration** – as much as what they tell – the **plot**.

Glossary

plot: what happens in the story

Getting you thinking

What actually **happens** in the following extract from Raymond Chandler's *The Lady In the Lake*? The 'I' narrator is the private detective Phillip Marlowe.

> 'You want to see me?' he barked.
>
> He was about six feet two and not much of it soft. His eyes were stone grey with flecks of cold light in them. He filled a large size in smooth grey flannel with a narrow chalk stripe, and filled it elegantly. His manner said he was very tough to get along with.
>
> I stood up. 'If you're Mr Derace Kingsley.'
>
> 'Who the hell did you think I was?'

How does it work?

All that **happens** is that Mr Kingsley asks if Marlowe wants to see him, and he says, if he's Kingsley, yes. But the **narration** conveys a lot more than that.

If Chandler was just writing **plot**, he might have written:

> 'You want to see me?' he said.
> 'Yes,' I answered.

But this misses the whole point of the novel – its **energy, wit and atmosphere**.

The **narrative** conveys that atmosphere: a hard menacing world where tough men talk – and act – tough. This type of novel is called the **'roman noir'**, the 'dark' detective novel.

Descriptive verbs like 'barked' and the tone of Kingsley's reply ('Who the hell did you think I was?') create the **noir** world.

Chapter 1 AF1 Write imaginative, interesting and thoughtful texts APP

Chandler's narrator **talks** to you in sharp, pacy American rhythms, with witty comparisons and a kind of world-weary streetwise poetry: 'His eyes were stone grey but with flecks of cold light in them', 'He was about six feet two and not much of it soft'.

The **dialogue** that follows the extract is like a shoot out:

> 'I don't like your manner,' Kingsley said in a voice you could have cracked a brazil nut on.
>
> 'That's all right,' I said, 'I'm not selling it.'

Now you try it

In pairs, decide what the basic **plot content** of the following extract is:

> I lit a cigarette and dragged a smoking stand beside the chair. The minutes went by on tiptoe, with their fingers to their lips...
>
> Half an hour and three or four cigarettes later a door opened behind Miss Fromsett's desk and two men came out backwards, laughing. A third man held the door for them and helped them laugh. They all shook hands heartily and the two men went across the office and out. The third man dropped the grin off his face and looked as if he had never grinned in his life. He was a tall bird in a grey suit and he didn't want any nonsense.
>
> 'Any calls?' he asked in a sharp bossy voice.

Development activity APP

Fill in and continue the following **narration** describing the secretary, Miss Fromsett, in a **noir** style.

> *She wore a steel-grey business suit and...*
> *The edges of the folded handkerchief in the breast pocket looked sharp enough to...*
> *She wore...*
> *Her dark hair was...*

In your continuation, include details of her skin, eyebrows, make up, etc.

Remember, your purpose is to **narrate a personality** that fits the **tough, wise-cracking world** of the noir novel.

Check your progress

LEVEL 5	I can write a story in an appropriate style
LEVEL 6	I can narrate a plot with energy and imagination
LEVEL 7	I can sustain convincing imaginative narratives

2 Write in character sustaining a role or voice

> **This lesson will**
> - help you to write as someone else, using an apt language and tone.

This means that you 'become' another person. It is a bit like playing a character in drama, putting on their language and way of speaking like you put on a costume. If you aim to write in another voice like this and only *mostly* achieve it, you are still writing at Level 6 – so aim high!

Getting you thinking

Look at these two monologue extracts. In pairs, act them out them to each other. Which of the two characters is most different from you?

Thomo *(just suspended from school for fighting)*

Watchit…! They call me Thomo. Me – I'm always in trouble. Can't resist a fight. I don't know why but I just see red. If somebody picks on me, I have to fight back don't I? Why should they pick on me? Why should they pick on me just 'cause I'm small?

Thomo's head teacher

I don't know what's happened. I've been a teacher for eighteen years now and there was a time when I used to enjoy my job. I used to feel I understood the children I taught. I could relax, have a joke, they'd tell me about themselves. But now it's different…

Take Craig Thompson for instance. He's waiting outside my office now for fighting. He's the tenth boy I've seen this week about causing trouble in school. I shall have to suspend him – have no choice, even though I know he's not a bad lad at heart.

- If you had to write an extension of these speeches, what would you focus on about each character's (a) use of language and (b) way of speaking?

Remember

This is the way you 'become' another person – putting on their language like a costume.

Now you try it APP

The head teacher's speech is written in a different style from Thomo's.

1 Think about the following suggestions and then add as many differences as you can find:

Chapter 1 AF1 Write imaginative, interesting and thoughtful texts

- chatty – or not?
- sentence length?
- questions?
- statements?

2. How do you think the head teacher feels about what goes on in the school?

3. Imagine you are the head teacher. Write a continuation of his speech here, in which he makes clear why he has to suspend Thomo.

   You could start:

   I shall have to play the part of the strict head teacher and suspend him because otherwise…

4. Now write a less certain continuation where he asks questions and is more personal. For instance:

   But why should I? Wouldn't it be a change to say, Thomo, here, have a cigarette…

   In both cases, it may help to improvise these speeches in role first.

Development activity

Look at this monologue – Lana is a teenager who has been picked up by the police for joy-riding.

> I hate it when they get you on your own. I just stare back at them. Don't say much. What do they want to know? Why I did it? Why I got in that car with Thomo and the others on Friday night? Nah – they're not interested even when I do tell 'em. Not in the real reasons – the boredom, the fact I can't go home 'cos they threw me out, that Thomo's my only real mate. There's this one social worker who's there sometimes. She understands, listens. But the rest are a waste of space.

- In pairs, role-play a **conversation** between the social worker and a colleague. Discuss Lana, and try to think the thoughts of the social worker and use her language. ('*I feel sorry for her – she's had it tough…*')

- Now **write a formal report** from the point of view of the sympathetic officer, analysing Lana and her problems. But remember that she will make decisions, make statements (using some long sentences) and report facts. She is in authority. ('*Following the accident on… I attended the police interview with Miss Lana Robbins. It was clear that…*')

Check your progress

LEVEL 5	I can write imaginatively and thoughtfully as someone else
LEVEL 6	I can assume and mostly sustain a convincing voice and viewpoint
LEVEL 7	I can adopt and completely sustain a distinctive individual voice and viewpoint

3 Write in a form and style that achieves the right effect

This lesson will
- help you to choose the right form and write in an apt style.

This means that you should vary your writing. You should have a range of **formal and conversational styles**. You should also make a **thoughtful choice of personal, impersonal and creative forms**. You should be **imaginative, even daring**, in your choice, in your effort to **interest** your reader.

Getting you thinking

The **form** of a novel is the **type** of story it tells. The **style** is **how** it is told: how it 'speaks' to the reader. Look at this opening of the novel *David Copperfield* by Charles Dickens. The narrator here is a Victorian gentleman-author, looking back. The **form** is the 'growing up' novel known as a **bildungsroman**.

Glossary

bildungsroman: an early twentieth-century German term for a novel about someone's formative years: literally, 'education-novel'

> Whether I shall turn out to be the hero of my own life, or whether that station will be held by anybody else, these pages must show. To begin my life with the beginning of my life, I record that I was born (as I have been informed and believe) on a Friday, at twelve o'clock at night. It was remarked that the clock began to strike and I began to cry simultaneously.

- What is the **style** here? **How** does the narrator tell his story?

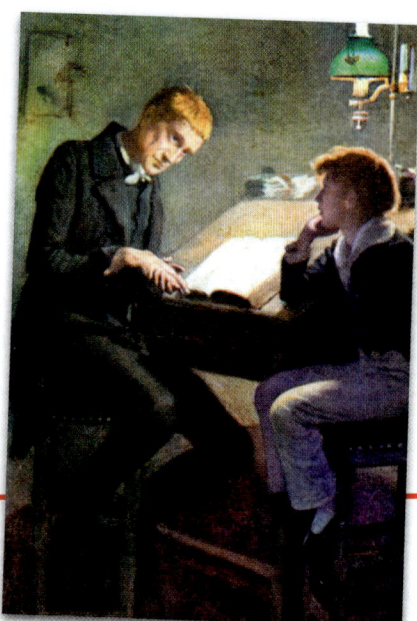

Now you try it

Not all **bildungsromans** are written in the same style. JD Salinger's novel, *The Catcher in the Rye*, is the narrative of a troubled late 1940s New York teenager called Holden Caulfield. However, it is still a **bildungsroman**, a 'growing up' story, and the narrator is still telling his own story.

Your teacher will show you the opening paragraph of this book.

Chapter 1 AF1 Write imaginative, interesting and thoughtful texts

1 Answer the following questions, giving examples.
- What differences do you find in the language and the way the narrator speaks to you?
- How does the author get you interested in his narrator?
- Is the narrator a convincing teenager? Does he speak like one?
- Does he send up adult formality?
- Does anything surprise you about the way he tells his story?
- Do you *like* the narrator? Is he funny?

2 What is the effect of the style? Why do you think Salinger created his narrator in this way?

3 What age or type of readers is the book aimed at?

Development activity

Remember

A writer always has choices like this to make and any good attempt at choosing an interesting form and style will get you a Level 6.

The school magazine has asked you to write about 'An Event that Changed My Life'.

Make a plan.

1 Decide: are you going to describe a **real event** or **imagine** one?

2 Now choose a form to suit.

If it's a real event, choose between:
- autobiography
- formal report
- diary
- any other suitable non-fiction form
- fact-based poem or play scene.

If it's an imaginary event, choose between:
- short story (describing that one event)
- extract from a bildungsroman
- extract from the autobiography of a made-up character
- any suitable fiction form (poem? play extract? other?).

3 Now decide on a style.

4 Now draft a plan of your account, with attention to form and style. Your teacher will give you time to **write this up in full** later.

Check your progress

LEVEL 5	I can develop and shape apt content for a purpose
LEVEL 6	I can choose and adapt an appropriate form and an engaging style for my purpose
LEVEL 7	I can mostly adopt, from an imaginative range, a form and style to fit my purpose

4 Write using a range of stylistic devices to create effects

This lesson will
- help you improve the vividness of your writing by thinking about sound, rhythm, setting and imagery.

This means that you try to make your writing vivid by thinking about the **sound**, **rhythm** and **picture** power of words. Just making a good attempt at creating the right effects is enough for Level 6 – so aim high!

Getting you thinking

Poetry is packed with word power and so writing poetry is a good training for all effective writing.

What do you notice about the **sound**, **rhythm** and **imagery** in this description of an armoured knight in winter? Pick out words, phrases or effects you particularly like.

> Dry clash'd his harness in the icy caves
> And barren chasms, and all to left and right
> The bare black cliff clang'd round him, as he based
> His feet on juts of slippery crag that rang
> Sharp-smitten with the dint of armed heels –
> And on a sudden, lo! the level lake,
> And the long glories of the winter moon.
>
> Tennyson, 'Morte d'Arthur'

How does it work?

The words **sound** like the thing they describe – the **clang of the armour** on rock (all the hard sounds: j, t, g, d and especially c). They contrast with the **long soft open sounds** (l and o) of the last two lines. This helps us **hear, in our mind's ear**, the knight emerging from the steep, dark, narrow rocks into the moonlit shore of the 'level lake.'

Lines encourage a poet to cut out verbal 'padding' and focus on the essentials. Even if you're not writing in verse, it is good to **cut out 'padding'** in the way **line-writing** encourages. And to use **words** that **sound right**. And to create **images** that **add** the right **pictures**.

Chapter 1 AF1 Write imaginative, interesting and thoughtful texts

Now you try it

Look at the comic panel of Thor and Reed Richards. A plain description of the action there might be:

> *Thor tries to hit Reed Richards but he stretches out of the way.*

Try using some **stylistic devices** to increase the effectiveness of this description. Include the THROKKK sound, either directly or by finding some real words which have 'thro' and/or 'k' sounds in them.

Find an **image (metaphor or simile)** that helps your reader **picture** Thor's slimy enemy, Reed Richards.

Try to suggest the **overall mood** of the **battle setting** by using **images** and **sounds** that fit. Use **repetition** and **rhythm** to **emphasise** this battle mood.

Now try to sum up **five features** of this battle scene in **five lines** of verse.

Development activity

Look online to find a picture of Munch's painting, *The Scream* (1893).

- How do you think the person pictured is feeling?
- What might have caused this feeling?
- How does the setting emphasise the feeling?

Imagine you *are* this person. Write some **lines of verse** (or **compact prose**) using **sounds** (**onomatapoeia** and **rhythm**) and **images** that convey **the scene** and your **feelings**.

Check your progress

LEVEL 5	I can use some imaginative detail and language in my writing
LEVEL 6	I can attempt to use a range of poetic devices to add impact and vividness to my writing
LEVEL 7	I can generally achieve impact and effect using a range of poetic devices

5 Make a good attempt to be creative with form

This lesson will
- help you to write with different levels of formality
- help you to write imaginatively – in a form that suits your purpose.

This means that you interest your reader by choosing an **apt form** for your material – but that you use this form in a **striking or even unusual** way. It is enough at Level 6 to make a decent **attempt** at such creativity.

Getting you thinking

In these opening verses of *Childe Roland to the Dark Tower Came*, the poet Robert Browning creates an imaginary world. A knight is on a quest to find a dark tower. He meets a 'hoary cripple' (an ancient, twisted man) who stops him and speaks to him.

> **Childe Roland to the Dark Tower Came**
>
> My first thought was, he lied in every word,
> That hoary cripple, with malicious eye
> **Askance** to watch the working of his lie
> On mine, and mouth scarce able to afford
> **Suppression** of the glee, that pursed and scored
> Its edge, at one more victim gained thereby.
>
> What else should he be set for, and his **staff**?
> What, save to waylay with his lies, ensnare
> All travellers that might find him posted there,
> And ask the road? I guessed what skull-like laugh
> Would break, what crutch **'gin** write my **epitaph**
> For pastime in the dusty thoroughfare,
>
> If at this **counsel** I should turn aside
> Into that **ominous tract** which, all agree,
> Hides the Dark Tower.

Glossary

Childe: an old word for knight

Askance: sideways, out of the corner (of his eye)

Suppression: the holding back

staff: a tall stick or crutch

'gin: begin

epitaph: the words on a gravestone

counsel: advice about which way to go

ominous tract: a scary track (with bad omens)

In pairs, decide how Browning
- addresses the reader (in what tone of voice?)
- lets you know this is a 'quest' story from the very start
- surprises the reader and creates suspense.

Chapter 1 AF1 Write imaginative, interesting and thoughtful texts APP

Now you try it

Look at this verse from later on in the poem. The rhyme words have been removed and listed in the table below.

> A sudden little river crossed my –
> As unexpected as a serpent –
> No sluggish tide **congenial to** the –
> This, as it frothed by, might have been a –
> For the **fiend**'s glowing hoof – to see the –
> Of its black **eddy bespate** with flakes and –

Glossary

congenial to: suited to
fiend: the devil
eddy: counter-current, swirl
bespate: flooded
wrath: anger
spumes: froth, foam

| comes | path | bath | **wrath** | **spumes** | glooms |

1. Checking with the rhyme pattern of the first verse, **insert these rhyme words** so that they make sense.

2. In pairs, decide what **words** in this stanza are suitably 'poetic' to describe this **strange quest landscape**. Which **words**, by contrast, are **chatty** and **everyday terms**?

Development activity

Choose your own form and style of writing to describe a key moment in a quest across a wasteland. You may want to find out more about the wasteland in Browning's poem or use others you know (like Frodo's quest across Mordor to Mount Doom) or want to make up.

Top tips

Choose suitable 'otherworldly' words and phrases.

Combine these words, phrases and features with at least some 'chatty' everyday expressions.

If you're using prose, try to	If you're using poetry, decide
• build in names of places or characters, or high-flown expressions familiar from myth and legend or sword and sorcery writing • but at the same time **talk** to your reader, as if having a casual word with a stranger.	• how many lines will go in your stanzas and roughly how long each will be – will they be of uniform length like Browning's? • will you have a rhyme pattern? (Browning repeats two rhymes three times each as follows: ABBAAB. It might be easier to have more rhymes or none at all!)

Check your progress

LEVEL 5 I can develop ideas at an appropriate level of formality
LEVEL 6 I can attempt to combine levels of formality in a text for creative effect
LEVEL 7 I can more or less consistently vary the level of formality within a text

Level Booster

LEVEL 5

- I can write imaginatively and thoughtfully and interest the reader
- I can plan, develop and shape my writing
- I can choose the right word, sentence, paragraph, text
- I can write vividly, powerfully, memorably
- I can develop a convincing viewpoint or role

LEVEL 6

- I can write with a clear emphasis on narration rather than plot
- I can write in character sustaining a role, voice or point of view
- I can write in a form and style that achieves the right effect
- I can write using a range of stylistic devices used to create effects
- I can make a good attempt to be creative with appropriate form.

LEVEL 7

- I can narrate stories with fluency and imagination
- I can usually sustain well-judged, distinctive individual viewpoints
- I can usually sustain a consistent and appropriate form, formality and style
- I can creatively apply the sound and picture power of language
- I can usually vary form, style and effect where appropriate

Chapter 2

AF2 Produce texts which are appropriate to task, reader and purpose

This chapter is going to show you how to
- Write imaginatively thinking about audience and purpose
- Use a range of techniques to create effects
- Write persuasively for a particular audience
- Adapt what you have read for different purposes.

What's it all about?

Understanding that written style must fit the needs of a specific audience.

1 Write imaginatively thinking about audience and purpose

This lesson will
- show you how to write for a particular purpose.

Being creative means using language to create interesting effects. But the effects must fit the purpose of writing. Rich imagery might suit a story or poem, but not a letter of complaint!

Ask yourself:
- What sort of language conventions are associated with my chosen text type?
- What good examples of this type of text have I read before? Can I 'borrow' any ideas to help me?

Getting you thinking

Why do greetings cards use verse? If you're expressing strong feelings like love, why might a short poem (like the one below) be better than, say, an essay?

Imagine you have been asked to write a love poem. You're going to look at two love poems and see what techniques these writers have used.

He Wishes for the Cloths of Heaven

Had I the heavens' embroidered cloths,
Enwrought with golden and silver light,
The blue and the dim and the dark cloths
Of night and light and the half-light,
I would spread the cloths under your feet:
But I, being poor, have only my dreams;
I have spread my dreams under your feet;
Tread softly because you tread on my dreams.

W.B. Yeats

In pairs
- Decide what strong feeling is expressed here.
- Decide who the poem is addressed to.
- Find three examples of where the poet puts his feelings across effectively. What words and images convey his emotion?
- Discuss the significance of the title.

How does it work?

Yeats is talking directly to the reader – this is a lover's address. Both the emotion expressed and the language used to express it are powerful, describing something fragile but magical.

Chapter 2 AF2 Produce texts appropriate to task, reader and purpose APP

Now you try it

Here is another love poem, this time by Robert Browning.

Meeting at Night

The grey sea and the long black land;
And the yellow half-moon large and low;
And the startled little waves that leap
In fiery ringlets from their sleep,
As I gain the cove with pushing prow,
And quench its speed in the slushy sand.

Then a mile of warm sea-scented beach;
Three fields to cross till a farm appears;
A tap at the pane, the quick sharp scratch
And a blue spurt of a lighted match,
And a voice less loud, thro' its joys and fears,
Than the two hearts beating each to each!

In pairs, discuss how the poet tries to capture your attention.

1 What emotions does the poem express? (Excitement, nervousness, intimacy?)

2 How does the poet convey these feelings? Think about the impact of
   - adjectives (are they simple or complex?)
   - **transferred epithets**
   - metaphors
   - the 'setting'
   - the 'story'
   - rhymes
   - the soundscape of the poem.

3 What mood is conjured by phrases like 'fiery ringlets' and 'warm sea-scented beach'?

Glossary

transferred epithet: here, 'startled' for waves: waves don't have feelings but the atmosphere of tension felt by the lover is described by describing the waves in this way

Development activity

Spread the love! Write a verse poem to go on a Valentine's day card. You will need to use language that suits a love poem, creates the right mood for the reader and fits onto a greeting card. Don't forget the impact of the title.

Check your progress

LEVEL 5	I can make the purpose of my writing clear throughout the piece
LEVEL 6	I can be creative when writing for a range of purposes
LEVEL 7	I can write in a sophisticated way for a range of audiences

2 Use a range of techniques to create effects

This lesson will
- help you select appropriate techniques to use in your writing.

A good writer needs to be aware of the different features and techniques that particular texts use. You then need to choose which of these techniques you will use to create a particular effect.

Getting you thinking

Read the following extract from *Misadventure in South-west China,* where Tim Nolen realises that his travels have taken a disastrous turn.

> By now I was exhausted from two straight days of grit and fuss. I sat on the edge of my seat, impatient and grumpy, wondering if it was really necessary to go through all this just to find serenity in China. At every little town we came to I asked the poor old man sitting opposite me if we were in Yangshuo yet. At dusk a series of strange, conical, rocky green hills started popping up in the distant sunset, looking more like cartoon drawings than anything real. After almost nine hours of bus travel I began to sense that the end was in sight; all I wanted was a plate of fried noodles, a big Qingdao beer, a shower and a bed.
>
> We arrived in Yangshuo to a fanfare of noise and lights. This was it! My man across the aisle suddenly seemed as excited as I was, as the bus driver slammed on the brakes. I leapt up, grabbed my backpack and fell out of the bus and onto the doorstep of the Zhuyang Hotel.
>
> 'Hello, welcome, my friend – you are tired, come inside!' shouted an exuberant Peter Xuehu, the chubby, middle aged proprietor. The bus roared off, and I stumbled inside as if disembarking from a week at sea. 'So, long trip, eh?' Peter Xuehu asked in good, if thickly accented English. 'Go upstairs to dorm at end of hall, take shower, pay me later!'
>
> I found the room, dropped my back pack, and reached for my money belt, only to feel the skinny slickness of my waist. With a sickening, heart-dropping horror, I suddenly realised that it was still tied to the overhead rack of the bus. No! I whirled about in a sudden panic and took quick stock of the predicament. Was this possible? I ripped open my back pack, as if I had put it there and forgotten – not there. What was in it? All my money, my passport, my plane ticket onward from Hong Kong, even my little Nikon One-Touch camera. Impossible! Defying all appeals to common sense, I had stashed every dollar, yuan, travellers cheque and credit card in the belt, with nary a penny in reserve elsewhere.

- What techniques does the writer use to get across the drama of the situation?

Chapter 2 AF2 Produce texts appropriate to task, reader and purpose **APP**

Now you try it

What happens next? Add an ending which explains whether he gets his belongings back or whether is he trapped in China with no money.

Try to use some of the techniques Tim Nolen used. For example:
- varied sentence length (slowing down the pace with longer sentences; picking up the pace with short sentences and lots of verbs)
- exclamations
- rhetorical questions
- alliterating adjectives.

Development activity

1 Think about a journey, trip or holiday when something went wrong. If you cannot think of a moment from your life, research recent news articles about travellers abroad to give you the basis for your story.

   Alternatively, interview a friend or family member. Ask them to tell you about an exciting or unusual travel experience they have had. Make sure you ask them enough questions so you are clear about what happened and how they felt.

2 Plan a piece of travel writing which captures the moment when things started to go wrong.
   - How will you give your piece an individual voice, like Tim Nolen's extract?
   - How will you make the reader share the emotions of the event?

3 Write your travel disaster story.

4 When you have finished, ask your partner to look at your writing and ask them to highlight the three best sentences. Then ask them to tell you where you could improve it. Ask them to be specific about the words and sentences they choose.

LEVEL 5	I can include a good range of different features for a piece of writing
LEVEL 6	I can use a good range of different features to create certain effects
LEVEL 7	I use techniques consciously and carefully to create deliberate effects

3 Write persuasively for a particular audience

This lesson will
- help you to use rhetorical devices to develop a persuasive point.

Some writing tasks ask the writer to develop and sustain a particular viewpoint, and to persuade others to share that viewpoint. This is especially true of speech writing. When making a speech, you need to think carefully about whom your audience will be, and how you can best appeal to them.

Getting you thinking

What makes an effective speech?

Read this extract from Barack Obama's speech, made on the evening he was elected as the President of the United States.

> If there is anyone out there who still doubts that America is a place where all things are possible, who still wonders if the dream of our founders is alive in our time, who still questions the power of our democracy, tonight is your answer.
>
> It's the answer told by lines that stretched around schools and churches in numbers this nation has never seen, by people who waited three hours and four hours, many for the first time in their lives, because they believed that this time must be different, that their voices could be that difference.
>
> It's the answer spoken by young and old, rich and poor, Democrat and Republican, black, white, Hispanic, Asian, Native American, gay, straight, disabled and not disabled, Americans who sent a message to the world that we have never been just a collection of individuals or a collection of red states and blue states.
>
> We are, and will always be, the United States of America.
>
> It's been a long time coming, but tonight, change has come to America… To all my other brothers and sisters, thank you so much for all the support that you've given me.
>
> I was never the likeliest candidate for this office. Our campaign was not hatched in the halls of Washington. It began in back yards, living rooms and front porches. It was built by working men and women who dug into what little savings they had to give $5 and $10 and $20.
>
> It grew strength from the young people who rejected the myth of their generation's apathy, who left their homes and families for jobs that offered little pay and less sleep. It drew strength from the not-so-young people who braved the bitter cold and scorching heat to knock on the door of perfect strangers, and from the millions of Americans who volunteered, organised and proved that more than two centuries later a government of the people, by the people, and for the people has not perished from the Earth.
>
> This is your victory.

Chapter 2 AF2 Produce texts appropriate to task, reader and purpose

In pairs, decide:
- What message is the speech trying to put across and why has it been written?
- How does Barack Obama appeal to his audience – and what different kinds of people does that audience include?
- What techniques are used to make this a powerful and persuasive speech?

How does it work?

In this speech, Barack Obama makes his viewpoint clear and appeals to his audience by
- setting out a **confident assertion** that in America everything is possible, then **giving examples** to reinforce this
- **making everyone feel involved** in his victory – using the pronoun 'we' extensively; emphasising that 'This is your victory', 'tonight is your answer'; thanking people for what they did to make it possible
- only occasionally using 'I' to subtly highlight his role in making these changes happen, without overemphasising it
- using **repetition**, **lists** and **the power of three** to emphasise and reiterate his points and make them sound persuasive.

Now you try it

Read the memo below.

> To members of the school council.
>
> There is a current debate in the media about whether students' education would benefit from a later start to school. Some 'experts' suggest that school should start at 11am, instead of before 9am.
>
> What are your views on this? Please read around the subject and prepare a short speech giving the views of your year group.
> The school's senior management will be present, along with three governors and parents of some Year 11 students.
>
> We look forward to hearing your views.
>
> Mrs Earlyriser (Head teacher)

Now read this article, giving one journalist's viewpoint on the proposal.

Starting school at 11am is just pandering to teenagers

A little bit of unpleasantness is part of what education should be about, writes Gill Hornby

Families with teenagers are getting on so well in Britain today. So what a bore that Dr Paul Kelley of Monkseaton High School has chosen this very moment to pop up with his Theory of the Teenager and the Lie-in to set us at each other's throats again.

Dr Kelley, a headmaster of radical views, is putting such faith in a trial by Oxford neuroscientists, with which his pupils were involved, that he is planning to reschedule his school's day so that teenagers no longer have to roll out of bed much before 11. The research indicates that they are not being lazy – absolutely not – but are biologically programmed to sleep: getting them up is injurious to their academic performance and health. He reckons his school will get more top grades if everyone takes it easy to round about lunchtime.

He's right of course. Having to get up to go to school is an unpleasantness, one of the few that are left. The rest have all been ironed out. Various electronic devices have killed off the threat of even a moment's boredom. Facebook means teenagers can socialise madly even when stuck at home. School shoes come with toys in them, medicine is delicious, even toothpaste tastes of bubblegum – because everything, at all times, must be Fun.

In that context, an alarm clock and a repetitive, yelling parent is, indeed, an anachronism. It's not an easy job, waking up teenagers, but at least it is finished by 8am. Dr Kelley's 11am start would make it difficult for a parent to have a job, or even younger children. Well, we'll just have to give them all up, I suppose.

This is the same headmaster who recently proved that a science GCSE could be taught to A* standard, in one day. That may be possible, but that's not 'education'. The point of a science lesson is to learn some science, not to swindle a quick qualification out of the system. And one point of a school and a timetable is to produce adults who can function in society; not an entire generation that has a string of A*s, but feels entitled to be buried in a duvet till lunchtime.

Telegraph.co.uk 9 March 2009

- In pairs, note down the different arguments for and against a later start.
- What is Gill Hornby's own viewpoint? How does she make this clear?

Development activity

- Decide on the viewpoint you want to adopt in your speech.
- Think about who your audience will be. How can you best tailor your argument and your speech to appeal to them?
- Now transform your ideas, using evidence from the news article, into the persuasive speech requested by the memo.
- Remember to look at the different rhetorical techniques Barack Obama uses in his speech to get the audience on his side, and try them out yourself.

Check your progress

LEVEL 5	I can keep the reader of my writing interested throughout the piece
LEVEL 6	I can engage the reader and make them react in a particular way through the way I write
LEVEL 7	I can make my viewpoint persuasive and use subtle techniques to influence the reader

4 Adapt what you have read for different purposes

This lesson will
- help you transform information in one text into one that has a different purpose.

Good writers are able to take a text and use material from it for a different purpose. For example, you might read an interesting fiction story and turn it into a news article. This involves thinking about the conventions of each form.

Getting you thinking

Read these two openings of texts about animal attacks.

A

Underpants shredded in fight with kangaroo

by Kathy Marks (10 March 2009, *The Independent*)

When Beat Ettlin was woken up by a dark figure crashing through his bedroom window at 2am, he assumed it was a burglar. Moments later, a 6ft kangaroo was bouncing on his bed. It was not a situation that Mr Ettlin, who lives in a leafy suburb of Canberra, the Australian national capital ever expected to encounter. So he and his wife, Verity Beman, and their nine year old daughter Beatrix, ducked under the sheets while the kangaroo – which seemed as terrified as they were – gouged holes in the wooden bed frame with its claws, leaving a trail of blood on the walls.

The roo, which had injured itself smashing through the 9ft window of the master bedroom, jumped on top of them repeatedly. Then it was off, bounding into 10 year old Leighton's room. 'There's a roo in my room,' shouted the astonished boy, from his bed. Mr Ettlin, a 42 year old chef, originally from Switzerland, said yesterday: 'I thought "this can be really dangerous for the whole family now".'

Spurred into action, he jumped the seven stone marsupial from behind and pinned it to the floor. Then, as the kangaroo flailed and lashed out, he grabbed it in a headlock and wrestled it into the hallway, towards the front door. Using a single fumbling hand, Mr Ettlin – wearing only underpants, which were shredded from the tussle – opened the door and shoved his adversary into the night.

Chapter 2 AF2 Produce texts appropriate to task, reader and purpose APP

B

Alex was about to swim forward when there was another movement just outside his field of vision. Whatever he had seen before had come back, swimming the other way. Puzzled, he looked up. And froze. He actually felt the air stop somewhere at the back of his throat. The last of the bubbles chased each other up to the surface. Alex just hung there, fighting for control. He wanted to scream. But underwater, it isn't possible to scream.

He was looking at a great white shark, at least three metres long, circling slowly above him. The sight was so unreal, so utterly shocking, that at first Alex quite literally didn't believe his eyes.

It had to be an illusion, some sort of trick. The very fact that it was so close to him seemed impossible. He stared at the white underbelly, the two sets of fins, the down-turned crescent mouth with its jagged, razor-sharp teeth. And there were the deadly, round eyes, as black and as evil as anything on the planet. Had they seen him yet?

Anthony Horowitz, *Skeleton Key*

For each extract, decide:
- What type of text is this?
- What techniques has the writer used to interest the reader? Find examples from the text to prove your point.

Now you try it

Look again at the description of the kangaroo attack. It has all the ingredients of an exciting short story.

1 If you were rewriting it as a short story:
- What additional information might you need to make up? What would you miss out?
- Which parts of the story would you slow down or speed up to engage the reader?
- Whose viewpoint would you tell the story from?

Discuss your ideas with a partner.

2 Rewrite the kangaroo attack as a short story. Think about:
- Which part of the story is the most exciting? How will you create and maintain tension?
- What techniques can you use from Horowitz's description of the shark attack?

	LEVEL 5	I can adapt what I have read in one form and use the information in a different way
	LEVEL 6	I can adapt features from different texts to make my work more effective
	LEVEL 7	I can transform whole texts into well-written texts with an alternative purpose

Level Booster

LEVEL 5

- I can make the purpose of my writing clear throughout the piece
- I can include a good range of different features for a piece of writing
- I can keep the reader of my writing interested throughout the piece
- I can adapt what I have read in one form and use the information in a different way in my writing

LEVEL 6

- I can be creative when writing for a range of purposes
- I can use a good range of different features to create certain effects
- I can create a point of view throughout my writing
- I can engage the reader by writing in an interesting way
- I can adapt features from different texts to make my work more effective

LEVEL 7

- I can write in a sophisticated way for a range of audiences
- I can use techniques consciously and carefully to create deliberate effects
- I can use unusual or imaginative word choices to make my meaning clear
- I can make my viewpoint appear persuasive and use subtle techniques to influence the reader
- I can transform whole texts into well-written texts with an alternative purpose

Chapter 3

AF3 Organise and present whole texts effectively

This chapter is going to show you how to

- Effectively control and sequence your work, thinking about the reader's reaction
- Use a range of features to signal the text's direction to the reader
- Develop clear and effective introductions
- Manage information, ideas and events to maximise the effect on the reader.

What's it all about?

Structuring your ideas for maximum impact.

1 Effectively control and sequence your work, thinking about the reader's reaction

This lesson will
- help you to learn how to structure your work effectively
- help you to learn how to write to achieve your desired audience reaction.

Whatever **genre** you are writing in, you should be thinking carefully about the effect you want your writing to have on your audience.

Getting you thinking

Read these scenes from the opening of Joe Standerline's play version of *Stone Cold* by Robert Swindells.

Scene 1

*The street. A litter bin. A yellow spot comes up on **Link**. He looks bored. His clothes are scruffy and he looks dirty. He takes a good look at the audience then speaks to them.*

LINK Have you ever sat and watched people, really watched them? They're all in their own little world. Now and then they'll let you in if they're feeling brave or if they think they know you. But the rest of the time you might as well be invisible.

A couple of passers-by walk right in front of him. One drops a crisp packet at his feet.

  See what I mean?

***Link** picks up the crisp packet to see if there's anything left inside. There isn't. he moves towards the litter bin. The lights fade.*

Chapter 3 AF3 Organise and present whole texts effectively

Scene 2

***Shelter**'s living room. There is an armchair, small table, standard lamp and fireplace. A doorway leads from this room to the bathroom and kitchen. There is a window with heavy, drawn curtains. A cat lies quietly in a basket in front of the fireplace. Above is hung a portrait of an old-looking soldier. **Shelter** enters with a bowl of tomato soup.*

SHELTER   *(thinking out loud)* Haven? … Home … House …

He sits down, puts his soup on the table and picks up a dictaphone and starts to record.

> Day one. Everything is ready. Practice mission executed successfully. Executed. *(Sniggers. There's a knock at the door. **Shelter** ignores it).* Only complaint at present time is constant pestering from man upstairs. Have now verified code name and will shortly post mission statement to relevant body. Operation to be known as …

He stops the tape for time to think. He ignores another knock at the door.

> Hostel?… Shack… Shed…

Another knock. He is slightly riled.

> Shelter! That's it. *(Recording it)* Operation Shelter! Perfect. Succinct, yet welcoming.

Switches the tape off and slurps a mouthful of soup. There's another knock. The soup drips from his mouth as he speaks.

> Get. Lost.

1 How does the playwright want us to feel about Link in the opening scene?

2 How does he establish Link's relationship with the audience?

3 How does he want us to feel about Shelter? How can you tell?

4 Think about the *structure* of the two scenes. How does the order in which they are presented – Link, then Shelter – affect the way we see the two characters?

Now you try it

Structure is all about how you choose to present ideas – the order in which, and the way in which, you reveal information.

You are going to write two connecting scenes for a play about the dangers of unhealthy living for teenagers.

1 First think about how you will structure the scenes. Here are two possible ways you could open the play:

> Structure 1
>
> Scene 1: a lazy teenager lying in front of the TV eating junk food
> On the other side of the stage, lights up on Scene 2: another teenager at a table eating a salad and reading a book.
>
> Structure 2
>
> Scene 1: a plump, middle-aged jogger, Big Joe, runs on to the stage puffing; and then leans heavily on a railing. He pulls out a packet of cigarettes and is about to light one. At that moment, a teenager, Young Joe – in fact, the man as a boy, thirty years or so earlier – comes up to him.
> Young Joe: You don't wanna do that.
> Old Joe: What's it to you, sunshine?

On your own, decide which of these structures has the best potential. Alternatively, decide on your own structure.

2 Next, think carefully about how you want your audience to respond to the characters. For each character decide
- what they say
- how they say it
- what they are wearing
- what the setting is like
- how you want the audience to feel about them.

Chapter 3 AF3 Organise and present whole texts effectively APP

3 Then, write the first two scenes of the play.

As you write your play, keep a log-book of your decisions – why you have chosen to write the scenes as you have done; what you revealed about each character and when. (Did you hold back information? Did you keep the audience guessing? Did you use contrasting scenes or ideas, as in *Stone Cold*?)

Development activity

Share your script ideas with a small group.

In your groups, explain how you structured your drama, and how you tried to get your message across.

If time allows, choose one or two of the dramas in your group and perform them.

Ask your audience to tell you how they responded to the characters and why. Was this what you were expecting? If not, how do you go about making that happen? Ask your audience what they think you should do to get across your objectives.

Write down these thoughts and redraft your work.

Check your progress

- **LEVEL 5** I can structure my work clearly
- **LEVEL 6** I can control and organise my work, thinking about the audience's reaction
- **LEVEL 7** I can skilfully manage information, ideas and events to achieve an audience reaction

2. Use a range of features to signal the text's direction to the reader

This lesson will
- help you to learn how to use writing techniques which will help the reader to understand what your purpose is
- help you to learn how to use structural devices in your writing.

It is really important when you write to use language and structure to steer your audience in the direction you want them to go.

Speeches are often written with the clear intention of making an audience react in a certain way. To do this the speech must use techniques to direct the audience.

Getting you thinking

Read aloud this extract from Earl Spencer's speech at the funeral of Princess Diana.

> I stand before you today, the representative of a family in grief, in a country in mourning, before a world in shock.
>
> We are all united, not only in our desire to pay our respects to Diana, but rather in our need to do so, because such was her extraordinary appeal that the tens of millions of people taking part in this service all over the world via television and radio who never actually met her feel that they too lost someone close to them in the early hours of Sunday morning.
>
> It is a more remarkable tribute to Diana than I can ever hope to offer to her today.
>
> Diana was the very essence of compassion, of duty, of style, of beauty. All over the world she was the symbol of selfless humanity. A standard bearer for the rights of the truly downtrodden. A very British girl who transcended nationality. Someone with a natural nobility who was classless and who proved in the last year that she needed no royal title to continue to generate her particular brand of magic.
>
> Today is our chance to say 'thank you' for the way you brightened our lives, even though God granted you but half a life. We will all feel cheated always that you were taken from us so young and yet we must learn to be grateful that you came at all.

- What techniques does Earl Spencer use to make an impact on his audience?
- How is he trying to make us think or feel about Diana?

Chapter 3 AF3 Organise and present whole texts effectively APP

How does it work?

Earl Spencer leaves the audience in no doubt who the subject of the speech is: Princess Diana's name is mentioned many times.

The opening paragraph is a **sentence in four parts**. It is a **list** that builds outwards from him to his family, to the country and finally the world. It draws together his personal grief with that of his listeners.

He moves from talking about himself ('**I**') in the first paragraph, to talking collectively about what '**We**' feel in the second paragraph. Finally, in the last paragraph he talks directly to Diana as '**you**' – a clever device which adds emotional power.

The **paragraphs are generally quite short**, and each one has a clear subject. In paragraph four he signals the topic of his paragraph clearly, 'Diana was the very essence of compassion, of duty, of style, of beauty', before elaborating on this further.

Now you try it

You are trying to get your class to vote for you in a school election. You need to write a speech explaining why they should pick you.

First, plan your speech. What persuasive techniques can you use? Think about

- **addressing your audience directly** as 'you'
- using **lists** (especially lists of three)
- using **personal pronouns** 'I', 'we'.

Now think about the structure of your speech:

- Will you begin by talking about yourself and then go on to explain what you will change at school? Or will you begin with the issues and come back to your role at the end?
- How can you build your speech to a climatic moment?

Remember to anticipate some of the questions that might be asked by your audience.

Development activity

Give your speech. Take feedback from your group on what kind of impact it made on them and how it could be improved.

LEVEL 5	I can link my paragraphs together to indicate the overall direction of the text
LEVEL 6	I can use a range of features to signal the direction of the text to the reader
LEVEL 7	I can use a variety of devices to influence the reader's response

3 Develop clear and effective introductions

This lesson will
- help you to learn how to write a clear, effective and engaging introduction.

The introduction to a piece of writing is very important as it signals to the reader what you are writing about. Many writers think very carefully about who their audience will be and exactly what they want their audience to think as they are reading.

Different styles of writing will require different types of introductions.

Getting you thinking

Look at the following opening of the novel, *Z for Zachariah*. Robert O'Brien is trying to grab the attention of his readers.

> May 20th
>
> I am afraid.
> Someone is coming.
> That is, I think someone is coming, though I am not sure, and I pray that I am wrong. I went into the church and prayed all this morning. I sprinkled water in front of the altar, and put some flowers on it, violets and dogwood.
> But there is smoke. For three days there has been smoke, not like the time before. That time, last year, it rose in a great cloud a long way away, and stayed in the sky for two weeks. A forest fire in the dead woods, and then it rained and the smoke stopped. But this time it is a thin column, like a pole, not very high.
> And the column has come three times, each time in the late afternoon. At night I cannot see it, and in the morning, it is gone. But each afternoon it comes again, and it is nearer. At first it was behind Claypole Ridge, and I could see only the top of it, the smallest smudge. I thought it was a cloud, except that it was too grey, the wrong colour, and then I thought: there are no clouds anywhere else. I got the binoculars and saw that it was narrow and straight; it was smoke from a small fire. When we used to go in the truck, Claypole Ridge was fifteen miles, though it looks closer, and the smoke was coming from behind that.
> Beyond Claypole Ridge there is Ogdentown, about ten miles further. But there is no one left alive in Ogdentown.

- What makes this an effective opening?
- What information does Robert O'Brien give the reader at the start?
- Why do you think he chooses to give this information?
- What information is *withheld* until the very end of the extract?

Chapter 3 AF3 Organise and present whole texts effectively APP

Now you try it

Compare this with the top half of a web page:

Like any text, it aims to engage your attention – but, how is it different from a story opening?

Discuss with a partner:

- Where does it begin? Who decides – you or the website designer? How?
- How does it engage your attention?
- Does it have *any* similarities with the novel?

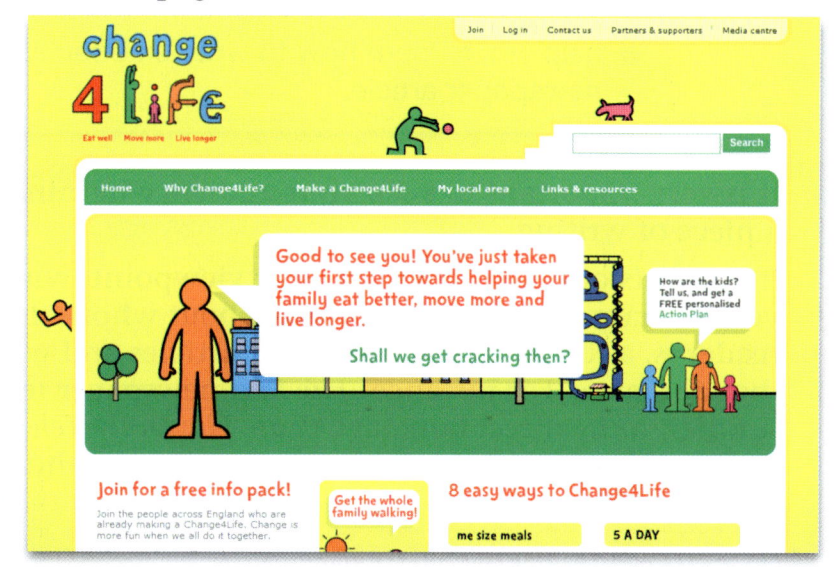

Development activity APP

Imagine you have been left alone, isolated in your town after a devastating attack/disease that has left everyone nearby dead.

EITHER…

1. Plan your own opening to a piece of creative writing in which you tell your story, revealing who you are, and where the events took place, what happened to other people, how you survived, and what happened to you.

   What information do you want your audience to know at the start? Don't give them too much information, as it will spoil the surprises for later on. You may choose, for instance, to delay telling them who you are or why you are alone.

   Play around with the structure of your work. You could use short paragraphs, like the extract from *Z for Zachariah*.

OR

2. Imagine the internet is still running after the event. Design a landing page for co-survivors which: welcomes them; gives advice on what to do; provides information, contacts etc.

   In both cases, consider what the 'opening' is and what it does: how it attracts or engages readers/users.

Check your progress

LEVEL 5	I can structure my work clearly
LEVEL 6	I can write clear opening paragraphs that introduce themes clearly
LEVEL 7	I can skilfully control the openings of my writing to influence the reader's response

4 Manage information, ideas and events to maximise the effect on the reader

This lesson will
- help you to learn how to organise your writing to make the maximum impact on your reader
- help you to learn how to write an effective tabloid-style newspaper article.

It is very important to keep your audience in mind throughout a piece of writing.

Journalists often write with a clear viewpoint, which they want you to share. They think carefully about whom their typical reader is, and tailor their language, articles and writing style to that audience. For instance, *The Sun* newspaper tends to use simpler, more direct language than *The Daily Telegraph*, for readers who want 'bite-sized' chunks of news and information.

Getting you thinking

Read the following article taken from *The Sun* newspaper (29 December 2008).

LOTTO BALLS-UP
Fury as ticket machines crash but draw goes on

LOTTERY chiefs were under fire last night for holding Saturday's draw despite a massive computer failure.

By Lucy Hagan

Nearly a million people couldn't buy tickets when shop machines crashed for four hours on Saturday.

Bosses of Lottery operator Camelot have no idea what caused the crash between 2pm and 6pm which also struck their website. The jackpot ended up **£800,000** lower than expected at £3.4 million – and many punters believe the draw should have been cancelled altogether or turned into a rollover.

But the BBC broadcast went ahead as usual, at Camelot's request. Host Carole Machin apologised for the glitch at the beginning of Saturday's TV show.

A Camelot spokesman said cancelling the draw was 'not considered' because problems were only 'intermittent'. He added: 'Lots of people had tickets and it would have been unfair on them to cancel it.'

But *The Sun* and Camelot were inundated with hundreds of complaints.

Rosemary Clarke, 65, of Cardiff said: 'It's disgusting.' Danny Edwards, 50, from Birmingham added: 'If they are not able to let everybody play, it's not a fair draw.'

Philip Munro, 42, from Ingatestone, Essex, said: 'It is unfair on people if they win and the jackpot is tiny.'

Camelot said the problem was fixed 90 minutes before the 7.30pm deadline to buy tickets.

Chapter 3 AF3 Organise and present whole texts effectively APP

How does *The Sun* get its message over to its audience?

Think about
- layout
- use of pictures
- the language used
- the structure of the piece
- the use of paragraphs
- use of bold letters
- use of capital letters
- how the ending of the article links back to the beginning.

Now you try it

Bring in a number of newspaper articles and compare how the writers have set out the articles on the page. Do you notice any features similar to the article on the lottery?

The following stylistic features are typical of a tabloid newspaper article:
- short, easy-to-follow paragraphs
- bold headline
- bold sub-heading
- bold opening paragraph
- photograph or other images
- writer's name
- use of quotations from people.

Development activity APP

Devise a tabloid-style article for your school newspaper on a current important issue in your school, for example: school dinners, a new sports hall, a school sports event, someone has won a prize for something or someone was caught cheating in a test.

Remember to present the article in the appropriate tabloid-style format.

You are aiming your article at students of a similar age, so remember to use appropriate language and presentational devices that will keep your audience interested.

Check your progress

LEVEL 5	I can clearly organise my writing into appropriate paragraphs across the whole text
LEVEL 6	I can control and sequence events and ideas taking account of the reader's reaction
LEVEL 7	I can skilfully shape information, ideas and events to get my intended purpose and effect

Level Booster

LEVEL 5

- I can structure my work clearly
- I can develop my material across the whole piece of writing
- I can develop clear links between my paragraphs
- I can make my ending link back to my opening
- I can organise sentences into proper paragraphs

LEVEL 6

- I can skilfully control the organisation of my writing
- I can write with a specific reader in mind
- I can use opening paragraphs to introduce themes clearly
- I can use linking devices between paragraphs
- I can anticipate what the readers' questions may be

LEVEL 7

- I can skilfully manage and shape information, ideas and events
- I can use introductions to influence a reader's response
- I can develop characters, plots, events and arguments clearly throughout the whole piece
- I can use a variety of devices to influence the reader's thoughts and feelings
- I can skilfully control how much information to give the reader and exactly when to do this

Chapter 4

AF4 Construct paragraphs and use cohesion

This chapter is going to show you how to

- Write an intriguing opening paragraph
- Use paragraphs to create a unity of theme in fiction
- Create a unity of theme in non-fiction
- Use bridges to link ideas between paragraphs
- Improve your ability to shape ideas into cohesive paragraphs.

What's it all about?

Using paragraphs effectively.

1 Write an intriguing opening paragraph

This lesson will
- help you make choices for effect when selecting between types of paragraph.

You are about to look at a paragraph from a successful nineteenth-century short story. The author is long dead, so we can get away with analysing his work critically. We can say what we like without any danger of him suing us!

Getting you thinking

Where do the two most important pieces of information or description come in the following paragraph? Think about:
- when we find the first key information about Isa Whitney
- when we see the sad effect of this on his life
- why Isa Whitney took the drug.

> Isa Whitney, brother of the late Elias Whitney, D.D., Principal of the Theological College of St George's, was much addicted to opium. The habit grew upon him, as I understand, from some foolish freak when he was at college, for having read De Quincey's description of his dreams and sensations, he had drenched his tobacco with laudanum in an attempt to produce the same effects. He found, as so many more have done, that the practice is easier to attain than to get rid of, and for many years he continued to be a slave to the drug, an object of mingled horror and pity to his friends and relatives. I can see him now, with yellow, pasty face, drooping lids and pin-point pupils, all huddled in a chair, the wreck and ruin of a noble man.
>
> Arthur Conan Doyle, 'The Man with the Twisted Lip'

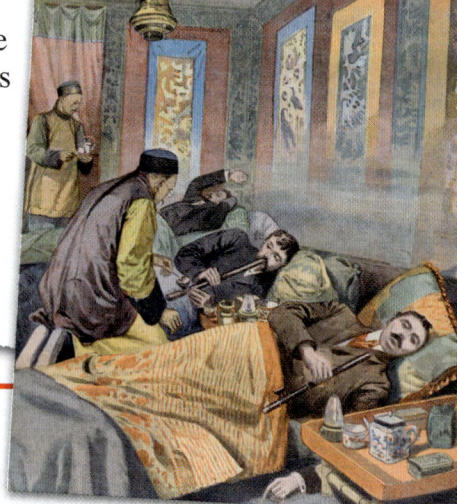

How does it work?

In both cases in this paragraph, the key information – relating to his addiction, and the effect – come at the end of longer sentences. In fact, the whole description depends on detailed, long sentences building up information and images of Isa Whitney.

First, the shocking fact of his addiction is withheld till the end of the sentence:

> Isa Whitney, brother of the late Elias Whitney, D.D., Principal of the Theological College of St George's was **much addicted to opium**.

Chapter 4 AF4 Construct paragraphs and use cohesion APP

Then, the shocking list of images is followed by the sad result of this addiction:

> I can see him now, with yellow, pasty face, drooping lids and pin-point pupils, all huddled in a chair, **the wreck and ruin of a noble man**.

Now you try it

1. First, try putting the last example into four separate sentences:
   - *I can see him now with his yellow, pasty face.*
   - *He had…*
   - *He would sit…*
   - *He was the…*

   Discuss with a partner which works better; the longer original, or the four short sentences?

2. Now have a go at writing your own extended sentences.

   Withholding information

   Add a shocking piece of information to this factual sentence:

   > *Our neighbour, Mr Cartwright, 52, a quiet, balding, unassuming man who was deputy manager of a local hardware shop, was also a…*

   Build a list of shocking images followed by the result:

   > *After he'd left, I could just make out his wife's shape, slumped in her wheelchair, in the rain-streaked conservatory, smoking endless cigarettes, a… and… woman.*

Development activity APP

Take either the Mr Cartwright and his wheel-chair bound wife, or another character you invent yourself. Create an opening paragraph for a story in which you

- start with a plain, factual description of someone and then add a surprise revelation
- develop some background information, which tells us more about the person and their situation
- finish with a powerful image or set of images and an observation from the writer about this person and their life or situation.

Finally, if you wish, develop the idea into a full short story.

Check your progress

LEVEL 5	I can invent and write about a character
LEVEL 6	I can develop information which tells the reader more about a character and his situation
LEVEL 7	I can write using powerful images about a character I have invented

2 Use paragraphs to create a unity of theme in fiction

This lesson will
- help you to know how to use paragraphs for effect.

When do you start a new paragraph? Identify the topic sentence in each of your paragraphs and check that every sentence relates to it. Ask yourself: can the paragraph be divided into smaller paragraphs with one theme in each paragraph? If your answer is yes, then divide the paragraph into smaller ones.

Getting you thinking

Look at the monologue below. Charles Dickens is speaking to an audience.

> Welcome ladies and gentlemen, welcome! I shall be most pleased to tell you something of my life.
>
> **1** Are you all aware that I was born in 1812, the year Napoleon invaded Russia? A cold, harsh winter it was, a winter that saw the French army decimated and the great Napoleon's men reduced to traipsing through the cruel snows of Russia, hoping to find their way back to France. **2** But enough of that, it was the year that gave birth to **me** – a winter of note! My early years were as harsh as the winter I was born. My father was a debtor. Like Mr Micawber, he was unable to make ends meet and was thrown into a debtor's prison. (pause) **3** Prison? How could my father pay his debts when he was cast into a place where he could not earn money? I saw, clearly, that reforms to the justice system were needed. I encountered injustices first hand. And then we moved to London and the debts mounted. My poor mother tried to start a school but she was too ill equipped and low on money. **4** My parents took me out of school and I was forced to work in a blacking factory. I cannot, even now, describe the agonies I endured there. I thought my life was wasted, my potential squandered by the monotonous, tedious work. **5** I felt trapped, humiliated, thrown out on the scrap heap. Ladies and gentlemen, that most terrible of experiences gave me my inspirations ... ideas for my poor characters, my imaginary children.
>
> Adapted from *Monologues with Duologue Activities*

This large paragraph can be split into five smaller paragraphs.
- Look at the numbering and see if you agree with these paragraph breaks.
- Look for the topic sentences in each numbered section and then reorganise the paragraphs.

Chapter 4 AF4 Construct paragraphs and use cohesion APP

Now you try it

Here is an extended dramatic monologue that hasn't been organised into paragraphs.

> As a street child there are but three places where I can lay my head on Her Majesty's streets. The first is the cold stone of the embankment near Waterloo Bridge. No gas-lamps reach there, nor the long, unfeeling arm of the law. There, I am safe. There, I sleep. There, 'though cold, I have rest. This is not like my second place. Sometimes the Bridge is too taken with other poor sleepers and I must seek refuge elsewhere. I go to Old Brompton cemetery. It is an hour's walk. It is a quiet, secluded place, and I have sleepers for company who neither snore, nor cry, nor prod me awake. Indeed, it is a place I know well for my own dear parents are buried there. Those sleepers have the deepest and warmest beds – the earth. The keeper locks the gates sometimes, 'though, and then I must seek other comfort. My third place of repose is the Royal Stables. I have a way with horses and if there is a kind stable-boy on duty I can plead a night's rest on a bed of warm straw. My companions there, gentle dappled mares and respectful stallions, watch over me. They are the only angels in my life.
>
> Mike Gould, *The Poor, Truthful Life of Hetty Marwood, aged 10½*

- Read the extract in pairs, then use your IT skills to split the monologue into four or five separate paragraphs.
- Rearrange the sentences to create a better **cohesion** between paragraphs.

Glossary

cohesion: connectedness, linking

Check your progress

LEVEL 5	I can rearrange the order of paragraphs
LEVEL 6	I can rearrange sentences and paragraphs for effect
LEVEL 7	I can rearrange sentences and paragraphs for emphasis, clarity and effect

3 Create a unity of theme in non-fiction

This lesson will
- help you write paragraphs with cohesion
- help you write paragraphs that flow.

When presenting an argument, remember that your reader does not know how it will develop. Your job is to guide your reader carefully, so that he or she does not need to make jumps between ideas.

Getting you thinking

Football is often described as the beautiful game. There have been many exciting moments and memories. But however good the players are, a team cannot do well without a brilliant manager.

There have been many great managers in football but the greatest manager, in my opinion, was Brian Clough.

Clough did not manage a rich and powerful team like Manchester United, Liverpool or Arsenal – he took over clubs such as Derby and Nottingham Forest. With Clough as manager, both clubs won honours they did not dream of winning before he arrived. Neither clubs have won honours since his departure.

Clough's teams were full of style, flair and they were irrepressible. Derby County won the league Championship under Brian Clough and Nottingham Forest won the European Cup twice. If Clough had managed Manchester United or Arsenal, his teams would have won every honour in sight.

This manager's greatness was to make something out of ordinary players. He turned them into stars! Some part of every player under Clough feared him, some part respected his quickness of mind and another part of a player responded to his encouragement.

- How does the writer make links between each paragraph?

How does it work?

The **end of each paragraph clearly links to the start of the next** as ideas are built up and extended.

Cohesion within paragraphs can be improved by the use of linking words (called **conjunctions** or **connectives**.) Examples of linking words and phrases are: such as, because, so, first, secondly, however.

Cohesion can also be improved by the repetition of key words and by replacing key words with **pronouns** such as it, they, these, this, that, he, she.

Chapter 4 AF4 Construct paragraphs and use cohesion APP

Now you try it

Look at the newspaper report below. The journalist is not pleased with her work and she knows Bernard Sheepshanks, the editor, will not be happy. In desperation, she turns to you for help.

Develop the article for her, so that old Sheepshanks will be pleased. You will need to add and alter paragraphs, trying to make links between paragraphs and create cohesion with linking words, repeated words and pronouns.

> At last, a British woman tennis player to be reckoned with.
>
> Laura Robson became the first British player to win the Wimbledon girl's title since 1984, when she beat Noppawen Levtcheewakarn 6-3, 3-6, 6-1. At fourteen years old, she has become the youngest winner of the girl's single title since Martina Hingis won in 1994 – the year Laura Robson was born!
>
> The strict training regime that all tennis players have to undergo has forced Laura to give up her favourite food – the pizza. Due to Laura's amazing victory, her mum felt Laura could have a pizza as part of her victory celebrations.
>
> Laura knows that, despite her Wimbledon win, she will need to work really hard to do as well as Martina Hingis, who went on to become the world number one female tennis player.
>
> Laura, as Junior Wimbledon Champion, will automatically enter the main Wimbledon draw next year; she could be playing against the likes of the Williams sisters or Maria Sharapova. Can she beat these world class players and one day win Wimbledon? We shall see!

Remember
The object of this exercise is to make your paragraphs flow using clarity of logic and unity between your paragraphs.

Top tips
To improve your work, it's a great idea to re-read your writing from the point of view of your intended audience. Who are your readers? The best way of doing this is to leave your writing for a day or two and then re-read. You can then redraft your writing, editing out bits that you feel do not work.

Development activity APP

Either research and write about the person you think is a brilliant manager in football or rugby, **or** write about a brilliant teacher who has motivated you.

Check your progress

LEVEL 5	I can write paragraphs that flow
LEVEL 6	I can write using clarity of logic between paragraphs
LEVEL 7	I can write using clarity of logic and unity between paragraphs

4 Use bridges to link ideas between paragraphs

This lesson will
- help you to sharpen the focus of your writing.

Most of us use simple bridges to link paragraphs. We often begin a paragraph with the word 'next' because we want to urge our reader on. However, the reader already knows it will be the next paragraph, because the page layout is already signalling this!

It is much better to use a variety of words and phrases, such as **furthermore**, **in addition**, **similarly**, **likewise**, **on the contrary** and **to sum up**.

Getting you thinking

Anyone Out There?

Many people believe there are aliens out there. They seem to interfere with human life. The Proof is that they have abducted people such as Betty and Barny Hill (1958). They've abducted people ever since!

Next, there is the question of crop circles. How did they form? Nobody knows! Its obvious that aliens created them, using their spacecraft in a special way.

And next, people who've been abducted have described the aliens who took them to their spacecraft. The most common alien known to man is The Grey. This alien is about two to four foot tall with a very large head and big, sunken eyes. The Grey has no hair. It does not show emotion. It seems cruel in the way it treats humans.

Next, Greys are known to be like dolphins. They have the same colour – grey!

Dolphins are believed to be creatures who once lived on land and they had legs – but at some stage in the past they returned to the sea and their legs became flippers. It is thought that in the alien world, these dolphin-like creatures stayed on land and became the dominant mammal.

- How could you improve the bridges in this paragraph?

How does it work?

The bad example can be turned into a good one by writing more complex bridges to link the paragraphs.

Paragraph Two – Furthermore,
Paragraph Three – In addition,
Paragraph Four – In fact,

Chapter 4 AF4 Construct paragraphs and use cohesion APP

Now you try it

Research and find out all you can about the Loch Ness Monster, the Bermuda Triangle or the Taos Hum. Write interesting paragraphs using complex bridges, such as:

Furthermore	In addition
On the contrary	To sum up
In fact	Similarly
Moreover	Finally
Likewise	

Development activity APP

When writing persuasive essays, you can use the following bridges

- to link paragraphs and to show addition – **furthermore, in addition, to add**
- to give examples – **for example, for instance, to illustrate, my point is …**
- to compare – **similarly, likewise**
- to contrast – **however, on the other hand**
- to conclude – **in other words, in conclusion, to sum up**.

Research, using the library, the internet and/or newspapers and magazines to find out all you can about bullying.

Then write a persuasive essay with the title '**Bullying of all kinds must not be tolerated**'.

Tips:
- **a** Think about definitions of bullying: physical, mental, cyber.
- **b** Stereotypes/myths.
- **c** Respecting differences.
- **d** Anti-bullying policy.
- **e** Pupil councils.
- **f** Making bullies change their minds.
- **g** Verbal threats.
- **h** Racial bullying.

Think about how you will link your paragraphs effectively, using bridges between one paragraph and the next.

Check your progress

LEVEL 5	I can write persuasive essays
LEVEL 6	I can write persuasive essays using my research notes
LEVEL 7	I can write persuasive essays using my notes and making at least eight different points

5 Improve your ability to shape ideas into cohesive paragraphs

This lesson will
- help you to sharpen the focus of your writing.

You will be investigating and presenting some facts about a situation for a particular audience. You will also make a recommendation at the end of your report, so will need to be very clear about how your ideas are connected together and lead to the conclusion.

Getting you thinking

Read the following report. As you do so, consider
- who has written the report
- who it is for (the audience)
- what its purpose is.

A Report on our form room, E 12

This report has been prepared in response to the request from Mr Wright, Head of Year 9. It considers the state of our form room, E 12.

Problems Concerning E 12

As a result of research carried out for this report, it has been discovered that E 12 has paint flaking off the walls. The two radiators fail to work and three windows are cracked and in a potentially dangerous condition. There are no curtains and blinds in the room and the video player does not work.

Possible Solutions

E 12 needs a complete makeover.

Recommendations

1. E 12 needs redecorating over the summer holidays.
2. The two radiators need immediate attention.
3. Three window panes need replacing.
4. All window areas need curtains.
5. The video player needs replacing with a DVD player.

Report prepared by Jake Winters.   Date 3-3-09

How does it work?

The **purpose** of the report is stated in the first sentence. The introduction tells the reader who requested the report and why. The third paragraph is written **after** the investigation into E12 and tells the reader the **findings** of the investigation.

Paragraph four presents the reader with the proposed action to be taken in a series of clear, numbered points.

Chapter 4 AF4 Construct paragraphs and use cohesion APP

Now you try it

Your school's head teacher wants to plan for the future, and has asked you to create a proposal for a 'Chill Zone' room or **suite** of rooms, which can be a place for pupils to go and quietly relax and reflect on work, relationships or problems. The **brief** given states that the 'Chill Zone' should be 'light, quiet and comfortable'.

First, **plan** your proposal by suggesting five sections and sub-headings. The headings will match the **subject** of each section. For example:

> Section 1: the purpose of this report
> Section 2: why the 'Chill Zone' is needed
> Section 3 etc.

You will need to shape your ideas rapidly into **cohesive** paragraphs. Remember, each new paragraph or section will need its own sub-heading.

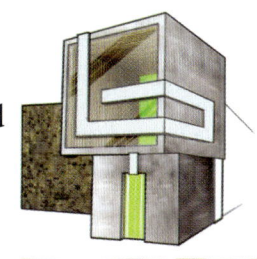

Glossary

cohesive: connected, hanging together well

Development activity APP

Research further ideas for your 'Chill Zone' proposal by using your own knowledge, talking to fellow students and teachers, and by looking at these websites which feature downloads from the Young Design programme:

http://www.imagineschooldesign.org/
http://www.thesorrellfoundation.com/publications.html

You will need to set out the report according to the planned headings you have decided upon.

You will also need to ensure that the language in your paragraphs is sufficiently professional and uses design vocabulary. For example:

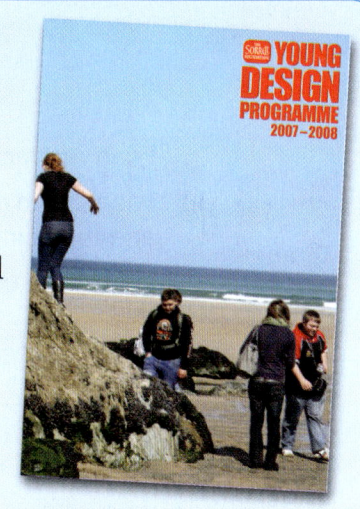

Adjectives to describe the feel and tone of the 'Chill Zone'	*bright and funky graphics, imposing steel, overhead beams*
Specific words to describe the space and building	*interior and exterior, inner, outer, eye-level, parallel, vertical*
Verbs to do with the movement of people in the space or the relationship between areas	*flow, connect, link, blur, merge with, lead to, descend, ascend, swing round*
Architectural terms	*atrium, dome, cube, zone, partition, wall, corridor*

Check your progress

LEVEL 5	I can write a report for a particular purpose
LEVEL 6	I can write a report using professional language
LEVEL 7	I can write a report using professional language and information gained from researching

Level Booster

LEVEL 5

- I can rearrange the order of paragraphs
- I can replace key words with pronouns
- I can write paragraphs that flow

LEVEL 6

- I can rearrange sentences and paragraphs for effect
- I can replace key words with pronouns for cohesion
- I can use bridges between paragraphs for cohesion
- I can create paragraphs unified around a theme or topic

LEVEL 7

- I can rearrange paragraphs for emphasis, clarity and effect
- I can improve cohesion of paragraphs by the repetition of key words and replacing pronouns for effect
- I can write using clarity of logic and unity between paragraphs

Chapter 5

AF5 Vary sentences for clarity, purpose and effect
AF6 Write with technical accuracy of syntax and punctuation

This chapter is going to show you how to

- Shape sentences for effect
- Write expressive and varied sentences in exciting descriptive writing
- Write effective dialogue in stories and scripts
- Use rhetorical devices to make an impact.

What's it all about?

Improving your use of sentences and using accurate sentences for effect.

1 Shape sentences for effect

This lesson will
- help you to vary the shape and structure of your sentences for effect.

The structure, length and word order of your sentences can all be used to have a particular effect on your reader.

Getting you thinking

Michael MacDonagh, a reporter for *The Times*, was in London on 4 August 1914 to record the start of the First World War. The German Army had invaded Belgium. To make them withdraw or face a declaration of war, Britain sent Germany an ultimatum which ran out at 11pm.

> At the approach of the decisive hour of eleven, we returned in our thousands to Whitehall. Then followed the slow and measured strokes of Big Ben proclaiming to London that it was eleven o'clock. We listened in silence. Was he booming out sweet peace and in red slaughter? No statement was made. There was no public proclamation that we were at war. The great crowd rapidly dispersed in all directions, most of them running to get home quickly and as they ran they cried out rather hysterically, 'War!' 'War!' 'War!'

How does Michael MacDonagh use different **sentence structures** to recreate the drama of this scene? Discuss the effects of the
- short sentences
- longer sentences, especially the second and the last sentences.

Now you try it

Think of a dramatic scene. It could be
- a road accident
- a great sporting moment
- a birth in your family.

You have six lines to describe it, using varied sentence patterns. Try to use
- longer sentences to set the scene and provide detail
- short sentences for emphasis or shock
- questions to express confusion or excitement about what is happening.

Chapter 5 AF5 Vary sentences   AF6 Write with technical accuracy APP

Development activity APP

The writer Richard Aldington served as a soldier in the First World War. In his novel *Death of a Hero* (1929), he describes the horrors of the Western Front, where he was gassed and suffered shell-shock.

Here George Winterbourne, the story's 'hero', explores one of the battlefields.

> All the decay and dead of battlefields entered his blood and seemed to poison him. At dawn one morning when it was misty he walked over the top of Hill 91, where probably nobody had been by day since its capture. The ground was a desert of shell-holes and torn rusty wire, and everywhere lay skeletons in steel helmets, still clothed in the rags of sodden khaki or field grey. Here a fleshless hand still clutched a broken rusty rifle; there a gaping, decaying boot showed the thin, knotty foot-bones. Alone in the white curling mist, drifting slowly past like **wraiths** of the slain, with the far-off thunder of drum-fire beating the air, Winterbourne stood in frozen silence and contemplated the last achievements of civilised men.

Glossary
wraiths: ghosts

1 First, look at Aldington's sentence structure in this passage.
   - What do you notice about a) the opening sentence and b) the final sentence?
   - Why does he delay the last clause of the final sentence? What is the effect?
   - What do you find effective in his description of the battlefield? (Think about word choice as well as sentence structure.)

2 Now imagine you have been asked to write a piece of **polemical** writing. In it, you will describe in detail a situation you feel strongly about. You need to make your own opinion clear. The situation could be
   - a modern war that you have seen on TV or read about in the press
   - the death of animals due to hunting or environmental damage
   - global warming.

Glossary
polemical: argumentative

Write a paragraph in which you try to
   - use '**fronted**' clauses and phrases ('Slowly, I realised …', 'When the war started, we all thought…')
   - **vary the word/clause order** of your sentences (Do you want to delay or build up to any important points?)
   - use **questions** ('How many more gorillas have to die before action is taken?')
   - use **short sentences** for emphasis or to clearly state a point.

Check your progress

LEVEL 5	I can vary sentence lengths and structures to give clarity and emphasis
LEVEL 6	I can use a variety of simple and complex sentences for effect
LEVEL 7	I can control a variety of simple and complex sentences for purpose and effect

2 Write expressive and varied sentences in exciting descriptive writing

This lesson will
- help you to use a range of sentence forms and features in exciting story telling.

A mixture of long and short sentences is a good way to make story telling exciting.

Getting you thinking

In Susan Hill's ghost story, *The Woman in Black*, Arthur Kipps is haunted by a sinister woman dressed in black Victorian clothes. At the end of the story, Kipps hopes he has escaped the woman but she reappears.

Read alternate sentences with your partner.

> And then, quite suddenly, I saw her. She was standing away from any of the people, close up to the trunk of one of the trees. I looked directly at her and she at me. There was no mistake. My eyes were not deceiving me. It was she, the woman in black with the wasted face, the ghost of Jennet Humfrye. For a second, I simply stared in incredulity and astonishment, then in cold fear.

- Can you find a **simple sentence**, a **compound sentence** and a **complex sentence**?
- Look at the first sentence. What is the key idea here? Why are two **phrases** placed before it?
- Look at the sixth sentence. What is the main idea here? Why are two **phrases** added? What is the effect of the short sentences and the longer ones?

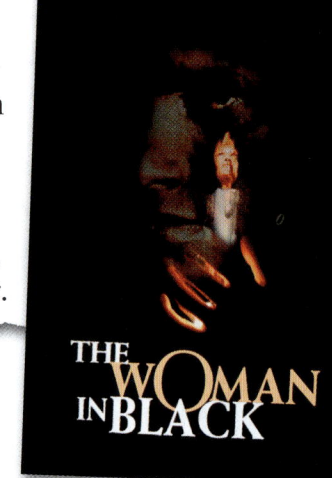

How does it work?

In complex sentences, writers add extra details to a simple sentence stem. Here are some of the most useful structures to try out:

1 **Conjuncts** (also called **fronted adverbials**) are useful to start a sentence:

then   however   by contrast   finally   similarly   furthermore   afterwards

2 **Prepositions** (little words that link nouns together: **in, on, by, to, from, after, until, beside, at**) can be used to start useful **prepositional phrases**.

> At twilight, I lay awake and waited.
> prepositional phrase

Chapter 5 AF5 Vary sentences   AF6 Write with technical accuracy APP

3 Subordinate clauses can act as **adjectives**, **nouns** or **adverbs**.

I admired Monet's picture, which was one of his last works.
                              adjectival clause describing 'picture'

That he completed this picture seems amazing.
        noun clause

He worked on it while he underwent eye surgery.
                   adverbial clause of time

These clauses may be placed at the **start**, in the **middle** or at the **end** of a sentence. It depends on where you want the main verb to have most impact.

Now you try it APP

Arthur Kipps first sees the ghost in a churchyard during a funeral.

> I half-turned, discreetly, and caught a glimpse of another mourner, a woman, who must have slipped into the church after we of the funeral party had taken our places and who stood several rows behind and quite alone, very erect and still, and not holding a prayer book. She was dressed in deepest black, in the style of full mourning that had rather gone out of fashion… Indeed, it had clearly been dug out of some old trunk or wardrobe, for its blackness was a little rusty-looking. A bonnet-type hat covered her head and shaded her face, but, although I did not stare, even the swift glance I took of the woman showed me enough to recognise that she was suffering from some terrible wasting disease.

If you analyse some of these complex sentences, you will be able to see how they add delicate detail to the main ideas.

Arthur Kipps sees the woman in black again near an empty house on a lonely island. She is standing among some graves beside a ruined chapel. It is a November afternoon at sunset. The only sounds are the seabirds, the waves and the wind.

Write four **complex** sentences about this meeting.

Here are four main verb units around which you might build the sentences:
- darkness was falling
- she stared
- I suddenly saw
- I was alone.

Development activity APP

Extend these sentences into a longer piece of writing.

Check your progress

LEVEL 5	I can use a variety of sentence lengths and structures
LEVEL 6	I can control a variety of simple and complex sentences for effect, especially in description
LEVEL 7	I can control simple and complex sentences for varied purposes and effects

3 Write effective dialogue in stories and scripts

This lesson will
- help you to write accurate and exciting dialogue and play-scripts.

Exciting stories almost always include dialogue. Dialogue tells us about the characters and their relationships and is an exciting way of moving the story on.

Getting you thinking

In the 'The Beast with Five Fingers' by W.F. Harvey, Eustace, a scientist, is sent the cut-off hand of his sinister dead uncle. Somehow the hand is alive and escapes from its box. It has one intention: to kill Eustace. Here he discusses the missing hand with his housekeeper, Morton.

> 'What was its colour?' asked Eustace. 'Black?'
> 'Oh no, sir; a greyish white. It crept along in a very funny way, sir. I don't think it had a tail.'
> 'What did you do then?'
> 'I tried to catch it; but it was no use… I think it must have escaped.'
> 'And you think it is the animal that's been frightening the maids?'
> 'They said it was a hand that they saw… Emma trod on it once at the bottom of the stairs. She thought then it was a half-frozen toad, only white.'

- With a partner, discuss which words and phrases describe the hand most effectively.
- Why do you think the writer chose to give us this information about the sightings of the hand in dialogue?

How does it work?

Remind yourself of the technical points about speech punctuation:
- Use single inverted commas.
- Each new speaker starts a new paragraph.
- Indent each new speaker by one tab. A lengthy piece of speech then returns to the margin.
- Check the positioning of commas, full stops and question marks in the passage above.

We don't speak in full, formal sentences. For dialogue to come alive, remember to use:
- **casual short forms** like 'don't'
- **speech tags** like 'Oh no' or 'Well, sir'
- **ellipses** (…) to show sudden breaks or pauses
- **adverbs and adverbial/adjectival phrases** to tell us **how** people speak.

Chapter 5 AF5 Vary sentences   AF6 Write with technical accuracy   APP

Now you try it   APP

Two maids at Eustace's house are discussing their sightings of the strange hand (helping with the washing up, running up curtains, attacking the cat etc.). Write their conversation.

You need to get the technical details right, but it should be exciting and frightening!

What personality will each character have? How will this affect what they say and how they say it?

Development activity   APP

Susan Hill also handles written conversation brilliantly. Here is an illustration. After a funeral, Arthur Kipps talks to a local lawyer about the mysterious figure that he saw in the churchyard.

> 'Tell me, that other woman…' I said as I reached his side. 'I hope she can find her own way home… she looked so dreadfully unwell. Who was she?'
>
> He frowned.
>
> 'The young woman with the wasted face,' I urged, 'at the back of the church and then in the graveyard a few yards away from us.'
>
> Mr Jerome stopped dead. He was staring at me.
>
> 'A young woman?'
>
> 'Yes, yes, with the skin stretched over her bones. I could scarcely bear to look at her… she was tall, she wore a bonnet type of hat… I suppose to try to conceal as much as she could of her face, poor thing.'
>
> For a few seconds, in that quiet, empty lane, in the sunshine, there was such a silence as must have fallen again now inside the church…

1. First, think about how the dialogue works.
   - What information is revealed in this passage?
   - How does the writer use dialogue to create surprise and suspense?
   - What do the words in between the speech tell us?

2. Now try writing a **radio script** that adapts and continues this conversation.

   Your script will be made up of dialogue: it won't have a narrator. How will you convey the information the book's narrator gives about each character – their thoughts and reactions – in your script?

   Don't forget the sound effects (feet on gravel, birds singing, jingling of the horse's harness etc.). In groups, try recording your script.

Check your progress

LEVEL 5	I can punctuate and set out speech accurately
LEVEL 6	I can use an expressive range of punctuation and sound layout in story dialogue or scripts
LEVEL 7	I can control speech punctuation and layout for varied purposes and effects

59

4 Use rhetorical devices to make an impact

This lesson will
- help you to shape sentences using **antithesis, repetition** or **balance**
- help you to think about the purpose and effect of such sentences.

Rhetorical devices can help you make an impact on your reader, whether you are writing fiction or giving a speech.

Getting you thinking

Read the opening of Charles Dickens' novel *A Tale of Two Cities*, about the French Revolution.

> It was the best of times, it was the worst of times, it was the age of wisdom, it was the age of foolishness, it was the season of Light, it was the season of Darkness, it was the spring of hope, it was the winter of despair…

With a partner:
- Pick out the patterns of three words that are **repeated** throughout to make a **balanced structure** for the ideas.
- Now find the pairs of words with **opposite meanings**.
- What does this sentence structure suggest about the French Revolution?

How does it work?

There are useful technical terms to describe these techniques:
- **antithesis** means contrasted ideas
- **repetition** means using the same word pattern again
- **balance** means one idea set against a second idea.

These are called **rhetorical devices** (**rhetoric** means 'the art of effective or persuasive speaking or writing'). They also create rhythms in your sentences, which will make them more enjoyable to read.

Now you try it APP

Rhetorical devices are crucial in **persuasive writing** or **speeches**. In these there are also other devices at work, such **rhetorical questions** that expect a certain answer, or **appeals for sympathy** ('My fellow Americans').

Chapter 5 AF5 Vary sentences   AF6 Write with technical accuracy   APP

In his 1945 satire, *Animal Farm*, George Orwell attacked the way that cunning political leaders used rhetoric to cheat ordinary people. An animal revolution at the Farm gets rid of the neglectful Farmer Jones. The pigs set up a new community in which 'All animals are equal'. Soon, however, they claim the best things on the farm (like the milk and apples) for themselves. Squealer, the pig propaganda chief, is sent to explain to the other animals:

> 'Comrades!' he cried. 'You do not imagine, I hope, that we pigs are doing this in a spirit of selfishness and privilege? Many of us actually dislike milk and apples. I dislike them myself. Our sole object in taking these things is to preserve our health. Milk and apples (this been proved by Science, comrades) contain substances absolutely necessary to the well-being of a pig. We pigs are brainworkers. The whole management and organisation of this farm depend on us. Day and night we are watching over your welfare. It is for *your* sake that we drink that milk and eat those apples. Do you know what would happen if we pigs failed in our duty? Jones would come back! Yes, Jones would come back! Surely, comrades,' cried Squealer almost pleadingly, skipping from side to side and whisking his tail, 'surely there is no one among you who wants to see Jones come back?'

1. Read the speech carefully. Find examples of the rhetorical devices discussed previously – and one or two more.
   - antithesis
   - lists of three
   - balance
   - rhetorical questions
   - repetition
   - appeals for sympathy

2. How does the last sentence work and why does it make an effective conclusion?

3. Now use these rhetorical devices to write your own short persuasive speech **for** or **against** a controversial topic. Ideas could include:
   - lowering the voting age to 16
   - electric v. petrol-driven cars
   - abandoning planet earth to live in space stations
   - single sex schooling.

   Try to use punctuation effectively in your sentences to create pauses, divide items in a list, or introduce a list of points.

> **Remember**
> **Semicolon: divides** lengthy items in a list, or balanced, contrasted statements in one sentence.
> **Colon: introduces** lists or material after sub-headings in notes or further explanation in detail of a general statement.

Development activity

In groups, or as a class, perform your speeches.

Check your progress
- **LEVEL 5** I can use a variety of sentence lengths and features to give clarity and emphasis
- **LEVEL 6** I can control a variety of sentence lengths use features, and some rhetorical devices
- **LEVEL 7** I can control varied sentence lengths and features, and use rhetorical devices effectively

Level Booster

LEVEL 5

- I can use various kinds of subordinate clause
- I can think about sentence length and structure, and about word order
- I can apply the forms and tenses of verbs
- I can use more complicated written speech
- I can use apostrophes for contraction and possession
- I can use colon and semicolon correctly

LEVEL 6

- I can understand main and subordinate clauses
- I can vary my sentence patterns
- I can use simple or compound/complex sentences for effect
- I can use written speech accurately
- I can avoid common mistakes of grammar and syntax

LEVEL 7

- I can construct a variety of sentence patterns for purpose and effect
- I can use a range of features to shape and craft my sentences
- I can use rhetorical devices like balance, repetition and antithesis
- I can control my punctuation, so that it is both correct and expressive
- I can control varied sentence lengths and features, and use rhetorical devices effectively

Chapter 6

AF7 Select appropriate and effective vocabulary

This chapter is going to show you how to

- Develop a varied, ambitious vocabulary
- Use vocabulary with subtlety and originality
- Choose vocabulary that is appropriate to your audience and purpose.

What's it all about?

Choosing the best words to enhance your work.

1 Develop a varied, ambitious vocabulary

This lesson will
- help you to build up a wider vocabulary.

It is important to develop your vocabulary so that you know a range of ambitious and imaginative words to use in your writing.

Getting you thinking

Look at these two versions of a piece of writing. The first is a Level 5, while the second has been rewritten to achieve a Level 7.

1. On Sunday, usually a boring day, we went to the fairground. As we walked up the hill I could hear music playing and people calling out happily. Walking over the hill, the fairground was an amazing sight: colourful lights shone and spun while children ran around, screaming with delight or chewing bright pink candyfloss. The smells were just as tempting. The scent of hot dogs drifted up to us, combined with the sweetness of toffee apples and fudge.

2. Sundays are usually grey, lifeless and boring. Like a snail, slowly heaving itself through thick mud, they seem to drag on interminably. However, last Sunday we went to the fairground. Trudging up Mixley Hill, I began to hear strange, tinny music calling to me, mingled with the happy cries of delighted children. I quickened my pace. The most amazing sight blazed before my eyes: a kaleidoscope of coruscating lights, spinning and merging in all the colours of the rainbow. The panoply of tempting smells was similarly enticing. The thick scent of hot dogs drifted up to us, carrying with it the sweeter aromas of toffee apples and fudge.

- Why is the second version better? (Hint: it is not to do with being longer but the way in which things are described.)

Chapter 6 AF7 Select appropriate and effective vocabulary APP

How does it work?

Notice the use of

- **metaphor** ('Sundays are usually grey') and **simile** ('like a snail')
- **extra detail**: 'scent' becomes 'thick scent'; 'music' becomes 'strange, tinny music'
- **more descriptive verbs and nouns:** 'drifted', 'trudging'; 'panoply'
- **more complex images** (Compare the first sightings of the fairground. The second one is a bit over the top, but so are fairgrounds!)
- **more unusual words:** 'interminably', 'coruscating', 'enticing'. (If you don't know what they mean that's okay: look them up and use them again!)

Now you try it

1. Using a thesaurus and dictionary, find a more ambitious alternative for each of these ten words:

    Verbs: eat; give; look; stop; think
    Adjectives: dark; dirty; happy; precious; red

2. Think about the different meaning that each of your new words brings with it. Then use your ten new words in an imaginative, entertaining paragraph or two.

Development activity APP

- Write a paragraph describing a tropical rainforest. Use your own wide range of vocabulary to create imaginative, ambitious descriptions. Also, try to use all of the words in the vocabulary bank below.

abundantly	= in great number (adverb)
effulgent	= shining brightly (adjective)
emerald	= green (adjective)
glimmer	= to shine (verb)
moist	= a bit wet (adjective)
myriad	= many (adjective)
tendrils	= the leafless shoots of a climbing plant (noun)
verdant	= green with vegetation (adjective)
vertiginous	= high enough to cause vertigo (adjective)
vividly	= colourfully (adverb)

Remember

Every time you come across an unusual word in your reading, look it up and find out what it means! Remember to use it in your own writing.

Check your progress

- **LEVEL 5** I can use a range of vocabulary to describe a rainforest effectively
- **LEVEL 6** I can use increasingly ambitious vocabulary to create interesting images
- **LEVEL 7** I can use a range of vocabulary to engage the reader with original, interesting images

2 Use vocabulary with subtlety and originality

This lesson will
- show you how to make your writing more subtle and original by describing mood and detail.

Writing with subtlety means carefully conveying moods and details. At different times you might be elaborate and dramatic or calm and reflective. By choosing your vocabulary carefully you can make your work that little bit different from everybody else's.

Getting you thinking

Read these two extracts.

A

A volcanic island thrown out of the earth's crust. What was deep is high. What was hidden is visible for all to see. The red peaks of Fyr are a landmark and a warning. No one knows when the island will erupt again, spilling itself in furious melt into the burning sea.

Arum lilies grow here, trumpets blaring light, gunpowder stamens and a flint stalk. The lilies of the field neither toil nor spin but from time to time they explode, strewing the ground with a **shrapnel** of petals; force, fuse, flower.

B

This has been a year of strange events: some wonderful, some terrible.

In the autumn a great wind swept through my garden one night, and toppled two oaks, three maples and a chestnut tree, all top-heavy with wet leaves, rooted in sodden earth. Had the gale come a week later the leaves would have been gone and the trees no doubt survived: a week earlier and the earth would have been dry and the roots steadier, and all would have been well. As it was, the chestnut crashed through the conservatory and set off all the alarms, which joined with the sound of the gale to frighten me out of my wits, so that I would have telephoned Carl, my ex-husband, and forthwith begged for his forgiveness and the **restoration** of his protection, but as the chestnut had brought down the wires I couldn't. By the morning the wind had died down and I, Joanna May, was my proper self again, or thought I was.

Glossary

shrapnel: fragments of a bomb thrown outwards by an explosion

restoration: returning something to how it was

- How is the mood of each extract different?
- What specific words or unusual images are used to create the mood and help you to picture the scene?
- What different details are picked out?

Chapter 6 AF7 Select appropriate and effective vocabulary APP

Now you try it

Aiming to create a calm mood, describe someone getting warm by an open fire.

Make your descriptions restrained, rather than dramatic, because the atmosphere is supposed to be peaceful. Remember to include some specific nouns.

Afterwards, share your work with your partner and discuss how you both tried to develop a feeling of warmth and relaxation. Who was most successful? Why?

Development activity APP

1. Working with a partner, one of you should describe a party at a house while the other describes the house the following morning. To start with, mind map the different moods that the two pieces of writing will create and the vocabulary (including specific nouns) that you could use.

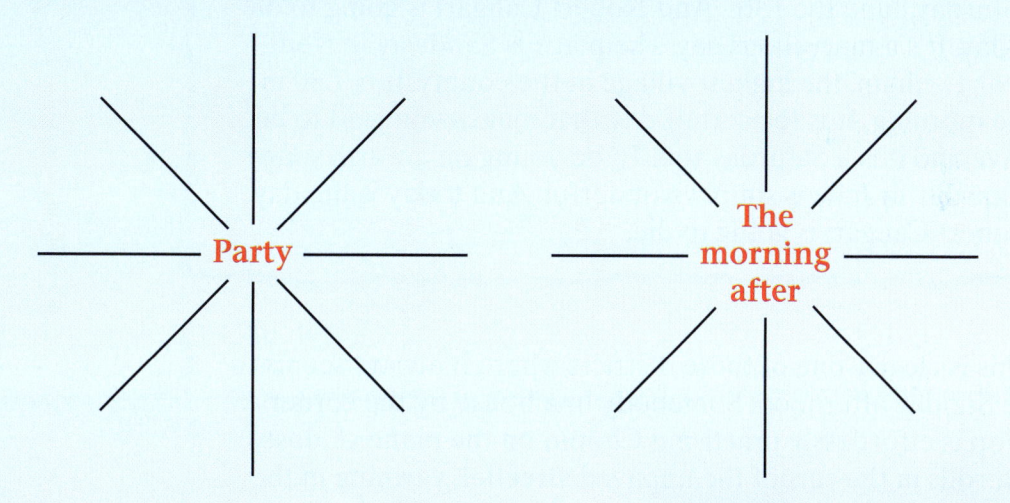

Party

The morning after

2. Having thought about the moods that you are going to create, start writing your description. Take your time to create imaginative and ambitious images. Write for 20 minutes, then share your work with your partner.

Top tips

To make a piece of writing subtle, consider the mood and specific details that you want the reader to imagine.

Don't go over the top with your vocabulary unless it suits the mood. Sometimes a few carefully selected images are much more effective.

Check your progress

- LEVEL 5 — I can create imaginative descriptions of the house
- LEVEL 6 — I can use some subtle vocabulary to convey the house and the mood effectively
- LEVEL 7 — I can fully convey the house and different moods with subtlety and originality

3 Choose vocabulary that is appropriate to your audience and purpose

This lesson will
- show you how to engage your reader and achieve your purpose through your selection of vocabulary.

In your work, you need to think about who you are writing for or to (**audience**) and what you are trying to achieve (**purpose**). These pages are about how to adapt your vocabulary so that it matches your purpose and audience.

Getting you thinking

Look at these two extracts: the first aims to entertain teenagers while the second informs and entertains older readers about life in Japan.

A

Saturday, June the 13th. And Robert Caligari is going to die today. It's a marvellous day. The place is Sandway in Kent, near Lenham, the highest village in the county. It is 7.30 in the morning. It is the sort of day that makes you glad to be alive and it is a Saturday too. To be young on a warm sunny Saturday in June is simply wonderful. And today is the day Robert Caligari is going to die.

B

This is clearly one of those districts where it always seems to be Sunday afternoon. Somebody in a house by the corner shop is effortlessly practising Chopin on the piano. A dusty cat rolls in the ruts of the unpaved **streetlet**, yawning in the sunshine. Somebody's aged granny trots off to the supermarket for a litre or two of honourable **sake**. Her iron-grey hair is scraped into so tight a knot in the nape no single hair could ever stray untidily out, and her decent, drab **kimono** is enveloped in the whitest of enormous aprons, trimmed with a sober frill of cotton lace.

Glossary
streetlet: a little street
sake: Japanese rice wine
kimono: a loose, ankle-length garment with wide sleeves, worn in Japan

- What differences do you notice in the vocabulary?
- How do the writers adapt their vocabulary to meet their purpose and audience?

Chapter 6 AF7 Select appropriate and effective vocabulary APP

Now you try it

Read the opening of Ian Fleming's *Casino Royale*, a spy thriller aimed at entertaining older readers.

> The scent and smoke and sweat of a casino are nauseating at three in the morning. Then the soul-erosion produced by high gambling – a compost of greed and fear and nervous tension – becomes unbearable and the senses awake and revolt from it. James Bond suddenly knew that he was tired. He always knew when his body or his mind had had enough and he always acted on the knowledge.

In pairs, discuss how it would need to be changed for much younger readers (8–10 year olds).

- What words or images might need simplifying?
- Are there bits you'd miss out?
- How would you keep it imaginative and entertaining?

Development activity APP

1. Choose one of the following products: a brand of perfume, a make of car, iPod, Nintendo Wii. In pairs, write the text for two adverts: one persuading teenagers to buy your product, the other persuading adults. What persuasive language could you use? How will you make the product sound wonderful? How will you specifically target your language at teenagers or adults?

2. Write the opening of a story aimed at teenagers. Choose either a romantic comedy about love and relationships or an action-packed adventure story. Think about the type of story, the kind of vocabulary you will use and how you will make it entertaining. When you have finished, read each other's stories and discuss your reasoning behind your vocabulary choices.

Remember

Always think about purpose and audience before writing and then choose appropriate vocabulary.

Check your progress

- **LEVEL 5** I can usually choose vocabulary to match genre and age group
- **LEVEL 6** I can select effective vocabulary to match genre and engage an age group
- **LEVEL 7** I can consistently use varied vocabulary to convey a genre subtly and engage an age group

Level Booster

LEVEL 5

- I can use a range of vocabulary effectively
- I can use vocabulary to create imaginative descriptions and convey ideas
- I can usually choose vocabulary that matches my audience and purpose

LEVEL 6

- I can use an ambitious range of vocabulary to achieve various effects
- I can use vocabulary with some subtlety and originality
- I can select effective vocabulary that matches my audience and purpose

LEVEL 7

- I can consistently use an ambitious range of vocabulary to achieve a very successful range of effects
- I can consistently use vocabulary to convey complex and thoughtful ideas with subtlety and originality
- I can consistently match my ambitious, effective vocabulary to my audience and purpose

Chapter 7

AF8 Use correct spelling

This chapter is going to show you how to
- Identify the building blocks of words
- Improve your spelling of ambitious, complex words.

What's it all about?

Perfecting your spelling.

1 Identify the building blocks of words

This lesson will
- help you to spell more complex words by visualising them.

As words become more complex, they often don't follow simple spelling rules. These pages are about exploring the building blocks that make up words. It can help you to try to visualise these when remembering a spelling. This doesn't mean spelling words phonetically (in other words, by the way they sound). Instead, try to visualise how the different syllables are spelled and then put them together.

Getting you thinking

Hor	ri	ble
Com	for	ta	ble
Tre	mend	ous
Mar	vell	ous
Sta	tion
Re	la	tion

How does it work?

Notice that different words contain similar syllable blocks. So the 'bull' sound in words like 'laughable' is usually spelled 'ble', while the 'shun' sound in words like 'attention' is usually spelled 'tion'. Getting used to recognising these different blocks and visualising them can help you with your spelling.

Now you try it

Break the following words into their syllable blocks: invest, person, rebel. Then see how you can alter the blocks to build similar words.

Chapter 7 AF8 Use correct spelling

For example, 'possible':

Pos	si	ble
Pos	si	bly
Pos	si	bil	i	ty
Im	pos	si	bil	i	ty

Once you have done this, choose three more words of your own to break into blocks and build new words from. Do any of your blocks contain similar spellings?

Development activity

1. Make a list of words that start with the following syllable blocks:

   at   el   head   mag   tel

   For example:
   attitude   electric   headstrong   magnify   telescope

2. Make a list of words that end with the following syllable blocks:

   tion   ious   ity   our   age

   For example:
   sensation   envious   enormity   harbour   baggage

3. As an extension, play a spelling game with your partner. Take it in turns to pick a word of more than two syllables and challenge your partner to spell it. Write out the number of letters as dashes, as if you were playing hangman. So, for example, xylophone:

   _ _ _ _ _ _ _ _ _

   If your partner gets it right straight away, they score five points. If not, they can keep swapping a point for a letter to help them. For example:

   _ _ _ _ P _ _ _ _

   See who manages to score the most points!

   If you don't know a word, try to break it down into syllable blocks and visualise the spelling.

Remember

The more times you see a word, the easier it's going to be to visualise it – so it's a good idea to increase the amount of reading that you do at home. (Whether you read novels, annuals or magazines, they're full of spellings that your brain will start to remember!)

Check your progress

- LEVEL 5 — I can spell the start and end of some complex words correctly
- LEVEL 6 — I can identify syllable blocks to help me spell most complex words correctly
- LEVEL 7 — My spelling is excellent, including complex vocabulary

2 Improve your spelling of ambitious, complex words

This lesson will
- help you to improve your spelling of more complex words.

When you start to use more ambitious, complex vocabulary in your writing, you probably won't know all the spellings. Some words you will have found in a thesaurus, but some you simply will have heard or remember from books. These pages are about checking spellings in a dictionary and trying to remember them.

Getting you thinking

In pairs, pick one column of words each. Spend 2 minutes trying to memorise these spellings (you might know some already). Then test each other. Which ones were the hardest? Did you find any special way to help you memorise them?

friend	buccaneer
guillotine	equilibrium
loquacious	onomatopoeia
somnolent	separate
tyrannical	voracious

Now you try it

Correct the spelling mistakes in this piece of travel writing. Use a dictionary to help you, and think about the different ways in which you could learn any new spellings that you find. Afterwards, challenge your partner to spell some of the words.

> From the remote, mist-shrowded mountins of the north, to the rich and fertile lowlands of the Mekong Delta, Vietnam is horntingly beautiful. Patchworks of briliant green rice paddies fade into the mountinus horrizon and reach down to the sweeping, desserted beaches caracteristic of the drammatic coasteline. Set in this seenically stunning land, the historic towns and sleepy fishing villages incapsculate the bygone charm of Asia's past. Friendly and incredibly hospittable locals invite you into their homes to sip tea and chat about life in their fasinating land. These chance incounters will leave lasting memmories that will forever tempte you to return.

Chapter 7 AF8 Use correct spelling APP

Development activity

Using a dictionary to help you, complete this crossword. Each clue gives you the first letter and definition of the word. As you work, try to remember what the words mean and how they are spelled.

Top tips

Get used to using a dictionary to check words!

Make up your own rules and reminders to help you spell complex words.

ACROSS

- 8 E. To put out.
- 10 L. Extremely comfortable.
- 12 J. Cheerful.
- 13 C. To consider something.
- 19 M. Concerned only with money and self-gain.
- 22 X. A plant able to grow in very dry conditions.
- 24 Y. A light sailing vessel.
- 25 I. New.
- 26 P. A ghost.

DOWN

- 1 S. At the same time.
- 2 N. A feeling of sickness.
- 3 R. Pains in the joints and muscles.
- 4 G. To shine, especially when wet.
- 5 K. Information gained from experience.
- 6 T. Irregular or disturbed.
- 7 O. To confuse or bewilder.
- 9 W. Twist as if in pain.
- 11 D. To speak badly of something.
- 14 A. Fake or man-made.
- 15 B. Polished.
- 16 U. Requiring immediate action.
- 17 V. Poisonous.
- 18 H. Clean.
- 20 F. From another country.
- 21 Z. Enthusiasm and hard work.
- 23 Q. Nicely old-fashioned.

Check your progress

LEVEL 5	I can spell common words, including most homophones, correctly
LEVEL 6	I can spell most words, including some complex vocabulary
LEVEL 7	My spelling is excellent, including complex, ambitious vocabulary

Level Booster

LEVEL 5
- I can spell common words and most homophones correctly
- I can use prefixes and suffixes correctly

LEVEL 6
- I can spell most words, including some complex vocabulary
- I can identify syllable blocks to help me spell complex words correctly

LEVEL 7
- My spelling is excellent, including complex, ambitious vocabulary

Teacher Guide

APP

Where the final task of the double-page section is substantial enough to provide a snapshot of students' progress, this has been marked as an **APP opportunity**.

Check your progress

Each double-page section ends with a **Check your progress** box. This offers a levelled checklist against which students can self- or peer-assess their final piece of writing from the **Development** or, occasionally, **Now you try it** section.

Level Booster

The end of chapter **Level Booster** is a less task-specific checklist of the skills students need to master to reach Level 5, 6 and 7. It can be used to help students see the level they are working at currently and to visualise what they need to do to make progress.

To the Teacher

The general aim of these books is the practical and everyday application of **Assessment for Learning (AfL)**: to ensure every child knows how they are doing and what they need to do to improve. The specific aim is to support **APP (Assessing Pupils' Progress)**: the 'periodic' view of progress by teacher and learner.

The books empower the student by modelling the essential skills needed at each level, and by allowing them to practise and then demonstrate independently what they know and can do across every reading and writing (APP) strand. They help the teacher by providing opportunities to gather and review secure evidence of day-to-day progress in each **Assessment Focus (AF)**. Where appropriate (and especially at lower levels) the books facilitate teacher **scaffolding** of such learning and assessment.

The series offers exercises and examples that we hope will not only help students add descriptive power and nuance to their vocabulary but also expand the grammatical constructions they can access and use: above all, the ability to write and read in sentences (paragraphs, texts) – to think consciously in complete thoughts. We aim at fuller, more complex self-expression – developing students' ability to express themselves simply or with complexity and the sense to choose when each is apt.

Each AF is a provisional isolation of various emphases, to be practised and mastered before bringing it back to the real reading and writing (of whole texts) in which all these – suitably polished – skills can be applied.

Gareth Calway

Series Editor

Chapter 1 AF1 Write imaginative, interesting and thoughtful texts

1 Write with a clear emphasis on narration rather than plot

How does it work?

Explain to students that the 'dark' **plots** in such novels are seldom clear – you never know whom you can trust or quite what is going on.' In fact, Chandler stated that his plots were just **an excuse to set up tough-talking dialogues** like the example. His plots are cryptic – even illogical – but his **atmospheres** are perfect.

Explain to students that *film noir* is the film version of *roman noir*. You could show them for interest a summary of Chandler's rationale in *The Simple Art of Murder*:

> But down these mean streets a man must go who is not himself mean, who is neither tarnished nor afraid…
>
> The detective in this kind of story must be such a man. He is the hero; he is everything. He must be a complete man and a common man and yet an unusual man. He must be, to use a rather weathered phrase, a man of honor – by instinct, by inevitability, without thought of it, and certainly without saying it. **He must be the best man in his world and a good enough man for any world.**

Now you try it

Remind students that the plot is just what actually happens.

Development

In pairs, students can read out their descriptions of Miss Fromsett. They should suggest improvements to each other and redraft the description.

Students can compare their own description of Miss Fromsett's eyes with Chandler's 'large dark eyes that looked like they might warm up at the right time and in the right place'.

2 Write in character sustaining a role or voice

Begin by explaining that in non-fiction writing, this would be 'adopt a viewpoint that isn't necessarily your own'.

How does it work?

Thomo's speech is written with the following features:

- chippy exclamation ('Watchit!')
- chippy rhetorical questions ('I have to fight back don't I? Why should they pick on me?')
- upbeat tone (all of the extract)
- direct simple statements ('They call me Thomo', 'can't resist a fight')
- repetition for emphasis and upbeat rhythm ('Why should they pick on me? Why should they pick on me just 'cause I'm small?')
- informal language – or 'colloquialism' (''cause', 'see red').

Explain that a **rhetorical question** is really a statement; it pretends to ask you something but doesn't expect an answer.

Draw out in discussion with students that all of these features come from first **imagining you are the person** and then **writing the way he would speak**. They won't be able to write him unless they think like him – **imagine they *are* him** – first.

Point out that whole novels can be written like this: narrated from a point of view and in a voice that is not the author's. *Catcher in the Rye* (in the next spread) is an excellent example.

Now you try it

Students should recognise that the head teacher feels things have changed in the eighteen years that he has been in the job. He is unable to relax and have a joke these days. There are more boys causing trouble.

Allow the students to work in pairs and discuss why they feel things have changed for the headmaster. Has society changed and have values changed? Or is the headmaster losing his grip?

Extension

1 You might like to set more able students the following task: Imagine you are Thomo. Write a monologue for him, in which he gives his view about Lana. Become him **in your imagination** first. Remember you're not a 'bad lad at heart' – you're small, always in trouble and you fight back when you're picked on.

Lana's your only mate too – but is she leading you astray, or you her? Do you want to help her with her situation at home, or just have a good time? You decide.

In your writing, try to sound like Thomo, asking 'why me?' questions and making simple statements

A really clever monologue would make it clear that under Thomo's brittle surface is a bewildered small boy.

2 The monologue of Colin is also worth sharing with students. He is a contrast to Thomo – a *really* bad lad, though he too has his reasons. ('You got to be liked').

> **Colin**
>
> It's tough here. You got to watch yourself. Things happen. There was this kid once – Justin. Right little weed, snivelling, right wimp. When he started moaning, you wanted to thump him, real hard, really beat him up. He was like that. Got on your nerves. No-one liked him. Not me. No-one. Even teachers didn't care for him. So one day we decided we'd had enough of friend Justin. We decided his number was up. So we done him.
>
> It wasn't just me. Whole bunch of us. We all planned it, when no-one was looking. He had this grotty little blue Raleigh. Remember it well. Didn't take much doing – we cut the brake wire. Even an idiot could've seen it. We gave him his chance.
>
> Then that evening after school he goes bombing down the hill like he always did. Only he couldn't stop, could he? Gets to the T-junction and – splat! Straight under a Ford Escort.
>
> It's like that this place. You got to be able to look after yourself. You got to be careful. You got to be liked.

The use of repetition and rhetorical questions (and even dark humour) here creates menace, in contract to Thomo's upbeat chirpiness. But it must be emphasised that the **imagination involved in these texts – the becoming of the character – takes primacy** here over any inventory of language features. The language features will follow if the character/voice is imagined as the student's own.

3 Write in a form and style that achieves the right effect

Getting you thinking

Allow students to work in pairs. Ask them to focus on the style of the novel. Ask them how the narrator tells the story. Would they have done it in a different way?

How does it work?

The style is **bookish**. The **narrator** uses **formal** words and phrases and **long complex sentences** to **address** (rather than **chat to**) his reader. ('Whether I shall', 'these pages', 'I record', 'I have been informed', 'it was remarked', 'simultaneously'.) It is a **literary language** and **style**. Even though he speaks directly to the reader, he does so in a very literary way.

Now you try it

Unfortunately, J.D. Salinger does not allow his work to be reproduced. Find the opening paragraph of *The Catcher in the Rye* and share it with the class.

Help students to appreciate that the **style** of a bildungsroman depends on **who is telling the story** and to **whom** (in other words, on whom the **intended reader** is).

The **narrator** is a **character** in both these bildungsromans. If the **author** himself were speaking, the form would be an **autobiography**. The forms often overlap though, and Dickens' first version of *David Copperfield* was an autobiography. He remains very close to the events described. Dickens wrote 'No-one can ever believe this Narrative, in the reading, more than I have believed it in the writing' (Charles Dickens, preface to *David Copperfield*, London, October 1850).

Allow students to work out the answers in pairs. When they have worked to a time limit, ask some pairs to present their answers to the group as a whole. There might be different answers, which could become part of an interesting class discussion.

Development

Point out to students that many novelists mix real and imagined events (as Dickens did) – they may decide to do the same.

Some forms demand a certain style (for instance, a formal report). Others – like a **bildungsroman** – depend on who is narrating and for what reader. (Remember *David Copperfield* and *Catcher in the Rye*.)

4 Write using a range of stylistic devices to create effects

How does it work?

Explain to students that the term for words or phrases that **sound** like the thing they describe is **onomatopoeia**.

The **rhythm** is a further effect of **sound**. The **rhythm** of the poem is **iambic pentameter** but 'Bare black cliff clang'd' puts four **stresses** together. This unexpected **change of rhythm** imitates the **hammering**.

The **setting** also suggests the knight's cold and lonely mood. So it is like an **image** (a **metaphor** or **simile**) for the knight's **feelings**.

Repetition – of **sounds** (and **images**, here of ice and dark and cold) – gives **emphasis**, helps your reader hear and see the loneliness.

Longer lines like the last two lines **can** have a different, more spacious feeling from shorter ones. **Short lines**, by contrast, often convey tension and excitement, or **finality**, like short sentences. But the long sentence of long lines leading up to the dash does not feel spacious or leisurely, the space is used to **pack in** lots **of action**. It is also packed full of sound effects and pictures.

Now you try it

Students should decide whether the lines of their poem will be long or short, end-stopped or open. Explain that **end-stopped** is when punctuation (especially a full stop) reinforces the end of the line; **open** is when the line end has no punctuation and the sentence continues through it. This is also called **enjambment**.

5 Make a good attempt to be creative with form

How does it work?

Explain to students that the word 'Childe' in the title tells us this poem is about a knight. And there are lots of 'otherworldy' and old fashioned words that conjure a faraway and long ago world.

But after that Browning keeps us guessing at least until the third verse, when we finally get the idea of a trail leading to the object of a quest (the Dark Tower). All we have until then is a spooky meeting in a deserted road with a menacing figure.

The way he tells this story is also surprising. We are having a casual conversation about something extraordinary – a **quest**. We might expect the language of the conversation to be, like the quest, **formal**, **symbolic**, even **distant**. And many of the words are. But the **way** we are spoken to – **the register** – is **casual**, almost **chatty**.

'My first thought was, he lied in every word', is directly addressed to us, the reader, as though the speaker knows us. There is no introduction – no 'My name's Childe Roland the Knight and this is my tale'. It is as if we are already in the middle of a conversation.

Explain to students that it is '**imaginative**' to play with a reader's expectations like this. In the same way, a poem is often better when your reader almost forgets the rhymes and rhythm patterns because he or she is grabbed by the subject or by the **way** you write about it. The rhymes and rhythms are still working their spell, but your reader's attention is on what is being said.

Development

Tell students that Browning's poem includes the following 'nightmare' features:

- bats
- a skeletal horse
- funeral banners
- weeds
- a black serpent-like stream
- thistles
- grass 'scant as hair in leprosy'
- toads in a poisoned tank
- bog, clay and rubble
- a huge black bird
- the noise of many bells
- a 'squat tower'.

The Dark Tower itself is imaginatively – because unexpectedly – dull and ordinary. But think of evil people you have seen pictured: Fritzl, Dr Shipman etc. Isn't the horror often how 'normal' they look?

Verse can give a built-in formality to your writing because it makes you choose language that fits a shape or pattern. But if so, try to blend it in with a more conversational **address** – a friendly and chatty way of talking to the reader.

Chapter 2 AF2 Produce texts which are appropriate to task, reader and purpose

1 Write imaginatively thinking about audience and purpose

Getting you thinking

Students should jot down their answers to the four questions. They might have the following answers:

- Love.
- His lover or the one he loves.
- a) Spreading heaven's cloths under her feet, b) The poet only has his dreams to give her, c) He does not want his lover to crush his dreams.
- The cloths of heaven are unattainable. He would give his lover the unattainable but he cannot.

How does it work?

The emotions expressed are powerful. The metaphor of somebody laying out their dreams for the beloved to walk on in this way is breathtaking because it makes the dreams sound fragile yet magical. Although it is a very short poem, the language is rich and ornate. Images of 'gold' and 'silver' give a sumptuous impression, as do the slightly archaic words like 'Enwrought'. The title suggests the lover's sense of longing and inadequacy.

Draw students' attention to the repeated words at the end of lines 'cloths/light/cloths/light/feet/dreams/feet/dreams'. What does this suggest?

What effect is created by the hesitant sound of the lines: 'The blue and the dim and the dark cloths/ Of night and light and the half-light'? Why does Yeats make these subtle distinctions between 'dim' and 'dark', or 'light' and 'half-light'?

Development

Encourage students to think about whom they are writing for and why they are writing. Is it to express their own strong feelings – to a particular person? Or is it to engage and interest other readers, perhaps to express feelings they can identify with? What kind of effect to they want to create: something tender, intimate or raw, or something funny?

Encourage students to choose their title carefully. What could it add to the meaning of their poem? You could give them this bank of possible titles to choose from:

> 'The lesson', 'Leap before you look,' 'First love', 'She walks in beauty like the night', 'This is just to say', 'Jealousy', 'Mirror', 'Valentine', 'Better to have Loved and Lost'

After they have written their poem, ask them to read it to a partner. Has the writer achieved what he or she hoped to? What do they like about it? Is there any thing they feel could be improved?

Students could also research some of the famous poems in the bank of titles. These will be easily found in poetry anthologies or on the internet by searching on 'poem' and the title. Students could select two poems that they particularly like and from them draw up some writer's tips. For example:

> *Tip 1: The title of the poem should highlight one of the reasons for writing it, or give the reader a clue about the feelings in the poem.*

2 Use a range of techniques to create effects

How does it work?

Writers try and create a particular effect with their writing. The writer here makes us feel Tim Nolen's tiredness and then his panic when he realises he has left all of his possessions behind on the bus!

Notice how he

- writes in the **first person** so we see events through his eyes and share his thoughts
- starts with a very **detailed description** of the tedium of the bus journey so we can share his impatience
- **builds anticipation** with hints of arrival and change from this monotony: 'green hills started popping up'

- **picks up the pace** in the second paragraph with short sentences, exclamations and verbs to suggest his speed and excitement ('slammed on the brakes', 'leapt up', 'grabbed')
- returns to his earlier fantasy of a shower and a bed in the fourth paragraph – it seems as if his dreams are coming true
- uses a number of techniques to highlight his panic in the fifth paragraph (vivid, alliterating **adjectives**: 'skinny slickness', 'sickening, heart-dropping horror'; **varied sentence structures and lengths** from rhetorical questions, one-word exclamations, to detailed description of his frantic search for the lost money belt).

Development

Research some other examples of travel writing such as Bill Bryson, Joe Simpson and Gerald Durrell. Add to your list of techniques and devise a top ten list for writing about places and exciting incidents.

3 Write persuasively for a particular audience

Getting you thinking

Remind students that speeches usually

- develop and maintain a clear viewpoint
- use rhetorical techniques to emphasise the important points
- make calculated appeals to their audience (or audiences).

If possible, show students video footage of the Obama speech before they read it: the speech can easily be found on YouTube. Ask them what they notice about the way the speech is delivered and the audience's reaction to it.

How does it work?

Barack Obama is making this speech to celebrate his victory in the election race, to thank all those who have made it possible in the election campaign, and to set out his vision for America.

He tries to appeal to a wide audience by making reference to people of all races, religion and age to make them feel involved in the success of his victory. He stresses that his victory was achieved by the efforts of ordinary American people.

He also acknowledges the historic nature of being elected as the first black President of the United States. Though his speech is deliberately inclusive, he makes subtle references to the civil rights movement who laid the foundations for this social change, borrowing the lyrics from Sam Cooke's song 'A Change Gonna Come', which was an anthem for the civil rights movement in the 1960s ('It's been a long time coming, but I know a change gonna come'). (The song was inspired in part by an incident in 1963 when Cooke and his band tried to register at a 'whites only' motel in Louisiana and were arrested for disturbing the peace.)

Students might be interested to learn that Obama uses several classical rhetorical techniques, known by their Greek names as

- **anaphora:** the repetition of a phrase at the start of a series of sentences ('It's the answer told by lines that stretched … It's the answer spoken by young and old…')
- **tricolon:** where a sentence is divided into a series of three ('If there is anyone out there who still doubts … who still wonders … who still questions…')
- **epiphora:** the repetition of a word or phrase at the end of a series of sentences ('tonight is your answer … This is your victory').

Development

Encourage students to think about the practical implications for the school of starting the day later: arranging school buses, the cleaning and management of the school, staff working hours, etc.

It might be fun for at least some of the class to perform their speeches. The rest of the class could take on the roles of the audience (the senior management team, three governors, the parents of some Year 11 students).

Extension

You could ask more able students to do the following tasks.

- Draw up some tough questions to ask journalist Gill Hornby about her views. See if you can successfully find holes in her argument. Role-play the conversation.
- Draft a letter in response to Gill Hornby's article / Dr Kelly's intentions, giving your opinion on the issue of late starts.

4 Adapt what you have read for different purposes

Getting you thinking

Allow students to work in pairs.

How does it work?

One text is a part of a children's adventure novel *Skeleton Key* by Anthony Horowitz and the other is from a newspaper article. Each extract would be written differently if they were re-created as a news article or an extract from a novel.

Now you try it

Allow students to jot down answers to this question. Students might think about how the Kangaroo got into the suburb and then why it decided to get into the house. They might add dialogue between Mr and Mrs Ettlin and their daughter, or focus on their thoughts and feelings as the injured Kangaroo rampaged in their bedroom.

The struggle between Mr Ettlin and the Kangaroo could be told through the eyes of a witness, perhaps the son.

Students might miss out some information concerning where the Ettlins live.

- Students may speed up the fight between Mr Ettlin and the kangaroo, and use short sentences to describe the struggle and to keep the action exciting. They may want to slow the action down as the kangaroo leaves the bedroom and heads for the boy's room. Longer sentences, to describe the departing kangaroo may be used in this section.

- Students could reasonably use any viewpoint, except Leighton's viewpoint, as he fails to witness the first part of the action. Alternatively, they could use a narrator's viewpoint. Some students might write about the events from the point of view of the kangaroo.

Development

- Imagine what happens to Alex after the shark incident. Hot seat Alex and ask him to recall what happened, how he felt and his strategy for survival.

- Using the kangaroo extract as a model, re-create the shark attack story as a gripping front page news report.

Chapter 3 AF3 Organise and present whole texts effectively

1 Effectively control and sequence your work, thinking about the reader's reaction

Getting you thinking

Explain to students that the play is about a homeless teenager called Link, and how he survives in London, and a psychopath called Shelter, who devises an evil scheme to get the homeless off the streets forever.

How does it work?

Draw out from students that the playwright has carefully ordered and juxtaposed these two scenes, so that we see Link first and begin to engage with him and feel sympathy for his situation. The shift to Shelter in Scene 2 is all the more shocking because we have been encouraged to identify with this homeless character, and understand his thoughts and feelings.

The playwright controls the audience reaction to the two characters through his use of stage directions, his sequencing of the scenes, and through the language each character uses.

We are encouraged to feel sympathy for Link. This is immediately shown by the fact that:

- he is dirty, bored and homeless
- people just ignore him and drop a crisp packet at his feet
- he obviously desperately needs food – he tries to find it in the empty crisp bag and then moves towards the bin at the end of the scene to look for food
- he talks to us directly, first taking a good look at the audience as if suspicious and wary.

In contrast, Shelter is presented as an unpleasant character from the start:

- he sniggers at the sinister word 'executed'
- his soup dribbles from his mouth as he speaks
- his rude 'Get. Lost.' which is made even ruder by the one-word sentences
- the scene is set perfectly to show his deceptive qualities, with thick curtains so no one can see inside his room. His comfortable surroundings are in direct contrast to Link's, which makes what he is planning seem even more malign.

Now you try it

How to set out the play

Using the *Stone Cold* play text as an example, try to ensure that your students:

- have character names in bold capitals
- put all stage directions either in brackets and italics for directions during lines, or only in italics between lines or for major directions
- have an introduction setting the scene at the start of the two scenes.

2 Use a range of features to signal the text's direction to the reader

Getting you thinking

Students should read the speech with care. They might like to read it through several times and practise reading the speech aloud, in pairs or in small groups.

Now you try it

Students should be reminded that to gain a good mark they should take note of the following points:

- They should speak clearly and loudly.
- They should speak at their normal pace – not too quickly or too slowly.
- They should vary the tone of their voice and avoid hesitations.
- It is important to keep eye contact with the audience.
- Students should think about their body language. It is better to stand up straight and appear confident.
- Finally, it is a good idea to use hand gestures – but only now and again.

Development

As students listen to the talks, they should take notes on how each speaker has dealt with the different features of their talk.

Structure – was it well organised, with a good strong start and end? How could it be improved?

Content – was the talk interesting? Why did the talk persuade you to vote for that person? Or dissuade you?

Volume and clarity – did the speaker vary his/her tone of voice? Did the speech have pace? Did the speaker look at and engage with the audience?

3 Develop clear and effective introductions

How does it work?

You may wish to discuss and explore the following ideas with your students:

- There is a lot of suspense created in this opening.
- The first two paragraphs are short, three-word sentences. This is to emphasise how afraid the narrator is and why he or she is afraid.
- We are not yet told anything about who the narrator is, why they are afraid or who is coming. This all adds to the tension, making us want to read on to find out the answers.
- The third paragraph gives us a little more information: that the narrator thinks that someone is coming, but they are not definite about it.
- The fourth paragraph begins to focus on the smoke and there is brief reference back to the past, 'last year', which we are told a little bit about, but there are many unanswered questions.
- The next two paragraphs develop the story further with references to the place names, the other sightings of smoke
- Finally, we are given the key information at the end of the sixth paragraph that there is no one alive in Ogdentown!

Now you try it

Explain to students that different styles of writing require different styles of openings. A story, a speech, a web page and a letter begin very differently as their purposes are often different. They all need to grab the attention of the reader, but whereas a story might reveal its key information slowly – which is part of its pleasure – an information web page needs to get you immediately involved in what it is offering before you click to a different page.

Development

1 Students may wish to plan their opening paragraphs by jotting down ideas and then trying them out with a partner. They can bullet point ideas or use a spider diagram.

2 If students decide to design a landing page, they will need to think carefully about presentation. They will need to plan their writing and the design. What typeface will they use? Will the writing be in colour? What drawings will they need for a high-impact web page?

4 Manage information, ideas and events to maximise the effect on the reader

How does it work?

Discuss the following points with your students.

The article gets straight to the main point in the first paragraph, summarising the story which is printed in bold letters to make it stand out. This allows readers who are scanning the newspaper quickly for stories to make a decision as to whether they want to read on. It also allows the writer to make the story interesting and exciting enough to persuade the reader to carry on reading. Why is the word **LOTTERY** in capitals?

The second paragraph develops the story further, explaining exactly why the lottery chiefs were under fire.

The third paragraph is longer than the first two as it now starts to build the story. The technique of **putting something in bold letters** has been used again to make the fact that the prize was **£800,000** less than normal stand out and seem more outrageous.

Notice how the ending of the article links to the beginning, as there is the comment about the lottery chiefs being under fire in the first paragraph, and four of the last five paragraphs have a list of the complaints.

The final paragraph says the problem was fixed in the end, bringing the article to a neat conclusion, resolving the key issue.

Now you try it

It is a good idea to bring in a range of tabloid newspapers.

Development

An interesting slant would be to take one of the issues and make it controversial.

Example:

TEST CHEATS
Year 9 Pupils to be Expelled

Chapter 4 AF4 Construct paragraphs and use cohesion

1 Write an intriguing opening paragraph

Getting you thinking

Students should quickly pick up that:

- Isa Whitney was addicted to opium.
- He became a slave to the drug.
- Friends and relatives pitied him.
- Opium changed the way he looked.

Students should realise that Isa Whitney wanted dreams and sensations like those that Thomas De Quincey had described.

Now you try it

Draw out with students that

- he had drooping lids and pin-point pupils
- he would sit huddled in a chair
- he was the wreck and ruin of a noble man.

Development

In pairs, allow students to bullet point ideas. Should students run out of ideas, they could use the following:

- The surprise could be that the person they are describing has no legs and/or is a drunkard.
- The character described could have been a soldier who had stepped on a land mine.
- There could be flashbacks to incidents in the character's earlier life.

2 Use paragraphs to create a unity of theme in fiction

How does it work?

Ask students: are there any sentences you could move around to create a better cohesion between paragraphs?

Model for students how these two sentences have been moved around. A better flow should have been created. Do they agree?

> I encountered injustices at first hand. I saw, clearly, that reforms to the justice system were needed.

Ask students if the above order is better than the original sentences in the monologue.

Now you try it

Explain that in a dramatic monologue, splitting the text into cohesive paragraphs can help to create pauses and focus the audience's attention.

Here, the skill will be not just to create new paragraphs, but perhaps to isolate specific sentences for effect.

Development

Ask students to do the following:

1 Write a monologue from either the cemetery keeper's, a policeman's or perhaps even one of the horses' points of view. Do they notice Hetty and other homeless children like her? How do they feel about them?

2 When you have written your first draft, look again at your monologue and see if you can rework anything. Are there any sentences that do not relate to the central theme of the paragraph? Can they be moved in any way or cut out? Redraft, using your IT skills.

3 The unity of theme in your paragraphs can be developed further by asking yourself the following question: Do the sentences which are not related to the central theme of your paragraph contain **vital** information?

   If the answer is no, cut them out. If yes, can the sentences be moved into existing paragraphs? Or can you create a further paragraph containing these sentences?

3 Create a unity of theme in non-fiction

Getting you thinking

The clarity of logic and flow of the passage is achieved by linking the paragraphs so that there is a clear theme running through each one.

- **Paragraph One:** This ends with the fact that teams cannot do well without a brilliant manager.
- **Paragraph Two:** Brian Clough is introduced as the example of a brilliant manager.
- **Paragraph Three and Four:** We learn what Clough's teams achieved.
- **Paragraph Five:** We discover how Clough motivated his teams. This links up with the first paragraph, which informed us that teams cannot achieve great things without a brilliant manager.

How does it work?

Ask students:

- What cohesive devices can you find in the passage above?
- Could any be added? For example, could the name **Clough** be replaced by **he** anywhere in the example passage?

Now you try it

Allow students to work in pairs. After a time limit, ask some students to report back and discuss the reasons for their changes. If there are different opinions, allow a discussion.

Development

Allow students to bullet point their ideas and show their plans to a partner before they write.

4 Use bridges to link ideas between paragraphs

How does it work?

See if students can link the paragraphs in the piece 'Anyone Out There?' by using other bridges not included in the examples.

Now you try it

Students can use the library or the internet for their research.

Development

Students should write their essays in rough, after planning the essays. Finally, they should redraft using their IT skills.

5 Improve your ability to shape ideas into cohesive paragraphs

Getting you thinking

Ask students to think about the following:

- A report has been written after a riot in a big city.
- A report has been written about a school's poor exam results.

In each case, who might write such a report? Who would it be for? What would be its purpose?

Allow students to discuss the questions. There may not be right or wrong answers.

Now you try it

Allow students to think about the report and then discuss in pairs.

Development

Students can set out their reports and make them look professional by using their IT skills.

End of unit fun

The class can play the paragraph game.

- In small groups of about five, decide on a story line. Work out who is writing the first paragraph, the supporting paragraphs and the final paragraph.
- Write your paragraphs, keeping to your agreed storyline.
- Read each paragraph out and see if they are cohesive. See if they can be used as one continuous story.
- Modify the paragraphs until you are happy with the story.

Chapter 5 AF5 Vary sentences for clarity, purpose and effect
AF6 Write with technical accuracy of syntax and punctuation

1 Shape sentences for effect

How does it work?

The writer has used sentence length and structure to capture the mood of the occasion.

The longer sentences at the start of the report build anticipation as the deadline approaches and crowds gather in Parliament Square. The two shorter sentences 'We listened in silence.' and 'No statement was made.' heighten the tension and draw our attention to what is said: nothing.

The writer uses a question to show the doubt and fear in the minds of the expectant crowd. From this moment of silence, the final long sentence rushes outwards, with the dispersing people and their cry of 'War!'

Help students to understand how the longer sentences are constructed.

- Ask students to look at the final sentence. Can they find the two subjects and verbs of the main clauses? ('The great crowd rapidly dispersed … they cried out')
- What other verbs can they find in the sentence? ('running', 'as they ran')
- Show them how the subordinate phrases and clauses ('most of them running…', 'as they ran') are built onto the main clause.
- Finally, ask, what is the effect of using a succession of verbs like this? How does it help to suggest the movement of the crowd?

It may be useful to remind students of some points about the grammar of sentences, covered in the Level 5 book:

- A **sentence is a group of words that makes full sense on its own**.
- A **simple sentence** is a single **clause**, which contains a **subject** (someone or something that does or is something) and a **predicate** (the other words in the clause, among which is a **complete verb**).
- A **compound sentence** contains **two or more clauses** of equal importance. They are joined by conjunctions (and, or, but, yet).
- A **complex sentence** has a **main clause** (the key idea) and one or more **subordinate clauses** (which are less important).
- A **phrase** is a group of words that does not contain a complete verb.
- Both subordinate clauses and phrases can act like **adjectives**, **adverbs** or **nouns** in a sentence.

All this sounds very dry and technical. However, the terms come alive when they are studied in actual writing by brilliant authors.

Now you try it

Here is a possible Level 6 answer:

A Road Accident

As the evening grew late, we flooded out of the cinema. The weather was dull and droplets of rain fell into the muddied puddles. Was that an old lady hobbling into the road? We watched her. Then the awful event. A screech of breaks, a thump and somebody was hurt – I could hear voices shouting 'Accident! 'Accident!' Accident!'

(Six sentences)

Development

You might want to look more closely at some of Aldington's **sentences** with the class to see how they work. Explain that the varied patterns make the meaning more subtle and expressive.

1. Aldington opens with a clear and confident compound sentence: 'All the decay and dead of the battlefields entered his blood and seemed to poison him.' The rest of the paragraph then adds detail to this statement, and builds up to his final conclusion.

2. Aldington adds extra description to a simple sentence stem with subordinate clauses:

   At dawn one morning when it was misty **he walked over the top of Hill 91**, where probably nobody had been by day since its capture.

   A phrase started (or fronted) by the preposition 'At' starts the sentence, and two adverbial clauses 'when it was misty' and 'where nobody had been by day since its capture' add to the meaning.

3. In the final sentence, the main clause is delayed and comes as a climax. He builds up to his angry and sarcastic point – that this devastating war demonstrates the 'last achievements of civilised man' – with a series of subordinate phrases.

   Alone in the white curling mist, drifting slowly past like wraiths of the slain, with the far-off thunder of drum-fire beating the air, **Winterbourne stood in frozen silence and contemplated the last achievements of civilised man**.

   He '**fronts**' the sentence with three **phrases**, one based on an **adjective** 'Alone', one on a **participle** 'drifting', and one on a **preposition** 'with'.

Students can write their polemical paragraph as a letter, a newspaper column or a piece of powerful descriptive writing like Aldington's.

2 Write expressive and varied sentences in exciting descriptive writing

How does it work?

Susan Hill's beautifully structured sentences of different lengths and patterns build up the tension and make the haunting very convincing. She uses a mixture of arresting short sentences and longer, complex sentences.

If necessary, remind students of the definitions of simple, compound and complex sentences.

A **simple sentence** consists of one **clause**. A clause contains a **subject** (someone or something) and a **predicate** (the other words in the sentence which include a **complete** or **finite verb**).

> The match started at two o'clock.
>   S   V   predicate

A **compound sentence** contains two or more clauses of equal strength, each with its subject and verb, joined by **conjunctions** (joining words like **and**, **but**, **or**).

> The players felt nervous but they were ready to play hard.
>   S   V   conjunction V   V

A **complex** sentence contains a **main clause** (the important idea) and one or more **subordinate clauses** or **phrases** (that depend on or explain further the main idea).

> Both managers, who were worried about their jobs,
> main clause   subordinate clause
> watched anxiously as the players ran out onto the pitch.
> main clause continued   subordinate clause

A **subordinate clause** contains its own complete verb. A **subordinate phrase** has no complete verb, although it may contain a **participle**, an incomplete verb form (going/gone).

Now you try it

A possible answer could be:

> Darkness was falling. I felt a presence in the half-light. Suddenly, I saw a woman with a terrible disease. She stared at me, moving slowly in my direction.

Encourage the students to

- use conjuncts (fronted adverbials) like 'slowly', 'suddenly' at the start of your sentences
- use prepositional phrases at the start of your sentences ('In the half-light, I…')
- include phrases or clauses that act as adverbs, nouns, or adjectives.

Development

Encourage students to think about what could happen next. Here are some possible ideas:

- Arthur Kipps realises he is alone, except for the ghostly woman in black.
- He moves towards her but she vanishes.
- He glances at the grave – it is the grave of a small child.
- The calling sea birds seem to mock him.

Ask them to now think of four more ideas.

3 Write effective dialogue in stories and scripts

Getting you thinking

Possible answers could include the fact that the hand is 'greyish white' and like a 'half-frozen toad'.

Now you try it

Here is a possible start.

> Ellen: Oh, Jane, I've seen that cold white 'and again!
> Jane: *(shocked)* I swear, we've got to get out of 'ere or we're goners.
> Ellen: I'm frightened. The last time I saw that 'and it was beckoning me to come into the parlour.

Continue the play…

Development

Encourage students to think about what happens next. Perhaps Kipps describes the woman in more detail while Jerome denies knowing anything about her.

Show students how scripts are set out.

- You put the character's name in the margin, followed by a colon.
- No speech marks are needed.
- Extra details of the character's behaviour or any background description go in brackets.

> MR. JEROME *(staring nervously)*: A young woman?
> *There is silence in the lane.*

Students could work in groups, to try recording their scripts. Share the best recordings with the class.

4 Use rhetorical devices to make an impact

Getting you thinking

- Students should pick out the patterns of these words as 'It was the …'.
- They should work out that the pairs of words are:

  best/worst

  wisdom/foolishness

  Light/Darkness

  hope/despair.
- Students will probably realise that the French Revolution offered hope and change but also foolishness and death.

Now you try it

1 Students should work in pairs and read the passage from *Animal Farm*. Several times.

2 Students should pick up that Farmer Jones is seen as the big evil baddie. The last line is an appeal and a threat. The worse thing (as the animals perceive it) is for Jones to take control of the farm again.

3 Students should plan their ideas before they write their speech.

Development

The class could – in groups or as a whole – choose a topic so that the speeches can be used in a group or class debate. Allow students to give feedback on each others' performance: whose rhetoric impressed? How could the speeches or their delivery have been improved?

Chapter 6 AF7 Select appropriate and effective vocabulary

1 Develop a varied, ambitious vocabulary

How does it work?

Allow students to look up words that they are not familiar with. They could then experiment with the words by writing a short sentence for each word, placing it in context and checking that it makes sense.

Now you try it

Once students have found their ambitious words, and written a creative paragraph or two, they could then read their writing to a partner. The partner could then suggest improvements to the paragraph.

Development

Students could write a short play about somebody trapped in a rainforest, using as many interesting words as they can.

Extension

An extension task for more able students who finish early:

Get into a group of three or four for a vocabulary game.

One person has control of the dictionary (take this in turns). The person with the dictionary picks a complex or unusual word at random.

The others in the group have to guess the meaning of the chosen word.

Once the meaning is understood, the others in the group have to try to use it in an imaginative sentence. The person with the dictionary chooses whose sentence is the most entertaining and effective.

2 Use vocabulary with subtlety and originality

Getting you thinking

Extract A is from a short story by Jeanette Winterson called 'Turn of the World'.

Extract B is from a novel, *The Cloning of Joanna May* by Fay Weldon.

How does it work?

Read the two texts aloud, then discuss them with the students. Try to draw out some of the following points:

Extract A is dramatic (thrown, spilling, explode). The words are often unusual (linking shrapnel to flowers) and suggest a strange atmosphere of beauty (light, petals) and danger (furious melt, burning). As well as the imaginative verbs, adjectives and adverbs, notice the use of specific nouns (arum lilies instead of, simply, flowers) to add finer distinctions.

Extract B is also dramatic (great wind swept, chestnut crashed) but is much more reflective (considering what *might* have happened), giving the writing a slower pace. There is a mood of uncertainty (or thought I was), with lots of contrasting language to emphasise this (wonderful/terrible, sodden/dry). Notice the specific nouns again (oaks, maples) and the use of everyday objects (telephone, conservatory, garden) to suggest realism and normality.

As a link to AF5, you could also discuss with students how (as well as the vocabulary) the length of the sentences helps to create atmosphere in each extract.

Now you try it

This task could be differentiated. Students sometimes find more dramatic writing easier to construct, so the less able could describe a house on fire.

Development

As an extension, play a 'mood' vocabulary game in pairs. One person should think of a mood, such as excitement. The other needs to come up with five words or descriptions that would fit that mood (for example: high-speed chase; rollercoaster; shrieking with glee; heart beating, pulse racing; galvanise).

3 Choose vocabulary that is appropriate to your audience and purpose

Getting you thinking

The first extract is from a novella by Tom Baker called *The Boy Who Kicked Pigs*. The second extract is a piece of travel writing by Angela Carter.

How does it work?

The first extract uses contrasting language and moods (die/marvellous) to create a shock and hook young readers. It also has a friendly tone (makes you glad to be alive) and simple but effective descriptions (to be young on a warm sunny Saturday).

The second extract paints a much more detailed picture for its older readers (dusty cat rolls in the ruts) and features more specific details and ambitious images (decent, drab kimono is enveloped in the whitest of enormous aprons). There is a friendly tone (somebody's aged granny) but more sophisticated references (Chopin). As a link to AF5, the class could also discuss the reasons for the different sentence lengths in each extract.

Now you try it

- Students should work out that they need to change some vocabulary such as 'nauseating' and phrases such as 'soul-erosion'.
- Students might wish to alter the last two sentences to make the story more imaginative and entertaining for younger children.

Development

As an extension to the first task, and a link to AF3, students could also discuss how they would use design and layout differently, according to the target audience, to present their text.

The second task is a good opportunity to challenge a more able group's perceptions of what appeals to boys and girls. As an extension, ask the class whether there was any pattern in which type of story the boys chose and which type the girls chose. Is this what they expected? Then get the students into mixed-gender groups of four. Ask them to discuss the kind of stories and vocabulary that they think appeals to boys and to girls. After this, feed back and discuss again as a class. Can we clearly define what boys and girls like to read? Have any students had their opinions changed?

Chapter 7 AF8 Use correct spelling

1 Identify the building blocks of words

How does it work?

Students can work in pairs to recognise the different building blocks.

Now you try it

Students can also try this example:

- Agree –
- Agree – able
- Dis – agree – able

Now find more words you can make from words with 'agree' in them.

Development

As an additional exercise, students can see how many dis- words they can make.

Examples:

Dis – cipline

Dis – tribute

2 Improve your spelling of ambitious, complex words

Getting you thinking

To help them with the task, the class could be reminded of the spelling mantra: look – think – say – cover – write – check.

How does it work?

Ask the class how well they did and what spelling techniques they used. Some of the words can be remembered by visualising their syllable blocks (for example: ty – ran – ni – cal). Others can be learned with a little saying (for example: 'there's a rat in separate' to make sure you don't get an e in the wrong place). For some of them, students could just learn the difficult part (for example: onomatopoeia is actually fairly easy until the end, so just learn 'poeia').

Now you try it

Students could rewrite the piece of travel writing, using their IT skills and making sure the spellings are correct.

Development

After the crossword exercise is complete, students can devise their own crossword.

Notes

Notes

Notes

Notes